PUFFIN BOOKS

UK | USA | Canada | Ireland | Australia
India | New Zealand | South Africa

Puffin Books is part of the Penguin Random House group of companies
whose addresses can be found at global.penguinrandomhouse.com.

www.penguin.co.uk
www.puffin.co.uk
www.ladybird.co.uk

 Penguin
Random House
UK

First published in the United States of America by Penguin Young
Readers Licenses, an imprint of Penguin Random House LLC,
and in Great Britain by Puffin Books 2017
001

Written by Jenne Simon

Printed in China

A CIP catalogue record for this book is available from the British Library

ISBN: 978–0–241–33768–4

All correspondence to:
Puffin Books
Penguin Random House Children's
80 Strand, London WC2R 0RL

MIX
Paper from
responsible sources
FSC® C018179

# The OFFICIAL
# COLlEGGTOR'S
# GUIDE

This book belongs to

**EGGSpert CollEGGtor**

Sophie

# WELCOME TO THE WORLD OF

HATCHIMALS
COLLEGGTIBLES™

21
**BUNWEE**
(ORANGE)

21
**BUNWEE**
(PINK)

22
**MOUSESWIFT**
(BLUE)

22
**MOUSESWIFT**
(YELLOW)

23
**SNAILTAIL**
(GREEN)

23
**SNAILTAIL**
(YELLOW)

24
**BEEBULL**
(PINK)

24
**BEEBULL**
(YELLOW)

25
**BUNWEE**
(YELLOW)

25
**BUTTERPUFF**
(PEACH)

26
**BUTTERPUFF**
(PINK)

26
**DRAGONFLIP**
(BLUE)

27
**DRAGONFLIP**
(PURPLE)

27
**FROWL**
(BLUE)

28
**FROWL**
(GREEN)

28
**MOUSESWIFT**
(MAGENTA)

31
**LAMBLET**
(BLUE)

31
**LAMBLET**
(PINK)

32
**PIGPIPER**
(PINK)

32
**PIGPIPER**
(YELLOW)

33
**PONETTE**
(ORANGE)

**PONETTE**
(PINK)
33

**CHICKCHAFF**
(ORANGE)
34

**CHICKCHAFF**
(RED)
34

**DONKEMU**
(BLUE)
35

**DONKEMU**
(PINK)
35

**LLAMALOON**
(PINK)
36

**LLAMALOON**
(PURPLE)
36

**MACOW**
(ORANGE)
37

**MACOW**
(WHITE)
37

**NIGHTINGOAT**
(BLUE)
38

**NIGHTINGOAT**
(TEAL)
38

**PONETTE**
(TEAL)
39

**PONETTE**
(BLUE)
39

## MEADOW .................................................. 41

**HEDGYHEN**
(GREEN)
42

**HEDGYHEN**
(PINK)
42

**KITTYCAN**
(BLUE)
43

**KITTYCAN**
(YELLOW)
43

**PUPPIT**
(BLUE)
44

**PUPPIT**
(PURPLE)
44

## JUNGLE .................................................. 46

**MONKIWI**
(BLUE)
47

**MONKIWI**
(PINK)
47

**PANDOR**
(BLUE)
48

**PANDOR**
(PURPLE)
48

**TIGRETTE**
(BLUE)
49

**TIGRETTE**
(ORANGE)
49

**ALBASLOTH**
(PURPLE)
50

**ALBASLOTH**
(PINK)
50

**ANTEAGLE**
(PINK)
51

**ANTEAGLE**
(PURPLE)
51

**CHAMELOON**
(BLUE)
52

**CHAMELOON**
(YELLOW)
52

**GORILLABEE**
(BLUE)
53

**GORILLABEE**
(PURPLE)
53

**PANDOR**
(TEAL)
54

**PARROO**
(RED)
54

**TIGRETTE**
(PINK)
55

**TOUCOO**
(BLUE)
55

**TOUCOO**
(PINK)
56

| | |
|---|---|
| CHIPADEE (ORANGE) 59 | CHIPADEE (PINK) 59 |
| DEERALOO (BLUE) 60 | DEERALOO (PINK) 60 |
| RASPOON (BLUE) 61 | |

CHIPADEE (ORANGE) — 59
CHIPADEE (PINK) — 59
DEERALOO (BLUE) — 60
DEERALOO (PINK) — 60
RASPOON (BLUE) — 61

RASPOON (PURPLE) — 61
SKUNKLE (GREEN) — 62
SKUNKLE (PURPLE) — 62
DEERALOO (MAGENTA) — 63
FOXFIN (PURPLE) — 63

FOXFIN (RED) — 64
HUMMINGBEAR (PINK) — 64
HUMMINGBEAR (PURPLE) — 65
MOOSEBEAK (BLUE) — 65
MOOSEBEAK (PURPLE) — 66

OWLING (PINK) — 66
OWLING (TEAL) — 67
POSSWIFT (MAGENTA) — 67
POSSWIFT (PURPLE) — 68
RASPOON (TEAL) — 68

DOLFINCH (BLUE) — 71
DOLFINCH (PINK) — 71
CRABLER (RED) — 72
CRABLER (YELLOW) — 72
DOLFINCH (TEAL) — 73

OCTAPITTA (BLUE) — 73
OCTAPITTA (PINK) — 74
PENGUALA (MAGENTA) — 74
SEASPOON (BLUE) — 75
SEASPOON (PINK) — 75

ELEFLY (BLUE) — 78
ELEFLY (GREEN) — 78
GIRREO (PINK) — 79
GIRREO (YELLOW) — 79
LEORIOLE (ORANGE) — 80

**LEORIOLE**
(PINK)
80

**ZEBRUSH**
(PINK)
81

**ZEBRUSH**
(PURPLE)
81

**CHEETREE**
(ORANGE)
82

**CHEETREE**
(YELLOW)
82

**DRAGGLE**
(PINK)
83

**ELEFLY**
(PINK)
83

**GIRREO**
(PURPLE)
84

**RHOOBY**
(BLUE)
84

**RHOOBY**
(PURPLE)
85

**ZEBRUSH**
(GREEN)
85

# DESERT ............................................................. 87

**KOALABEE**
(BLUE)
88

**KOALABEE**
(PURPLE)
88

**ARMADILLARK**
(GREEN)
89

**ARMADILLARK**
(YELLOW)
89

**CAMELARK**
(MAGENTA)
90

**CAMELARK**
(YELLOW)
90

**KANGAROOSE**
(BLUE)
91

**KANGAROOSE**
(PURPLE)
91

**SANDSNAKE**
(BLUE)
92

**SANDSNAKE**
(GREEN)
92

# RIVER ............................................................. 94

**FLAMINGOOSE**
(MAGENTA)
95

**FLAMINGOOSE**
(PURPLE)
95

**HIPHATCH**
(BLUE)
96

**HIPHATCH**
(PINK)
96

**SWOTTER**
(PURPLE)
97

**SWOTTER**
(RED)
97

**BEAVEERY**
(ORANGE)
98

**BEAVEERY**
(TEAL)
98

**DUCKLE**
(BLUE)
99

**DUCKLE**
(GREEN)
99

**FIGEON**
(BLUE)
100

**FIGEON**
(ORANGE)
100

**FLAMINGOOSE**
(FUCHSIA)
101

**FLAMINGOOSE**
(PINK)
101

**HIPHATCH**
(PURPLE)
102

**PLATYPIPER**
(GREEN)
102

**PLATYPIPER**
(PINK)
103

**SWOTTER**
(BLUE)
103

## SPECIAL EDITION POLAR PARADISE

 **POLAR DRAGGLE** 106

 **POLAR FOXFIN** 106

 **POLAR HUMMINGBEAR** 107

 **POLAR PENGUALA** 107

 **POLAR SEALARK** 108

 **POLAR SWHALE** 108

## SPECIAL EDITION LILAC LAKE

 **LILAC BUNWEE** 111

 **LILAC GIRREO** 111

 **LILAC HEDGYHEN** 112

 **LILAC PENGUALA** 112

 **LILAC SWHALE** 113

 **LILAC TIGRETTE** 113

## SPECIAL EDITION GIGGLE GROVE

 **GIGGLING DRAGGLE** 116

 **GIGGLING ELEFLY** 116

 **GIGGLING PANDOR** 117

 **GIGGLING PENGUALA** 117

 **GIGGLING RASPOON** 118

 **GIGGLING ZEBRUSH** 118

## LIMITED EDITION CLOUD COVE

 **CLOUD DRAGGLE** 121

 **CLOUD KITTYCAN** 121

 **CLOUD LEORIOLE** 122

 **CLOUD PIGPIPER** 122

 **CLOUD PONETTE** 123

 **CLOUD PUPPIT** 123

## SPECIAL EDITION SNOWFLAKE SHIRE

 **SNOWFLAKE BELUGULL** 126

 **SNOWFLAKE HUMMINGBEAR** 126

 **SNOWFLAKE NARWARBLER** 127

 **SNOWFLAKE PENGUALA** 127

 **SNOWFLAKE SEALARK** 128

 **SNOWFLAKE WALWREN** 128

# LIMITED EDITION MAGICAL MEADOW ....................................... 130

**MAGICAL BUDGIBY** (Yellow) 131

**MAGICAL BUDGIBY** (Green) 131

**MAGICAL FARROW** (Pink) 132

**MAGICAL FARROW** (Green) 132

**MAGICAL HAMSTAR** (Blue) 133

**MAGICAL HAMSTAR** (Pink) 133

**MAGICAL KITTYCAN** 134

**MAGICAL PUPPIT** 134

# SPECIAL EDITION GLITTERING GARDEN ....................................... 136

**GLITTERING ALBASLOTH** 137

**GLITTERING CRABLER** 137

**GLITTERING DUCKLE** 138

**GLITTERING PLATYPIPER** 138

**GLITTERING RHOOBY** 139

**GLITTERING WALWREN** 139

# SPECIAL EDITION CRYSTAL CANYON ....................................... 141

**CRYSTAL BEAVEERY** 142

**CRYSTAL BUTTERPUFF** 142

**CRYSTAL CHAMELOON** 143

**CRYSTAL FOXFIN** 143

**CRYSTAL POSSWIFT** 144

**CRYSTAL OCTAPITTA** 144

# SPECIAL EDITION CITRUS COAST ....................................... 146

**CITRUS ANTEAGLE** 147

**CITRUS BUTTERPUFF** 147

**CITRUS DRAGGLE** 148

**CITRUS MOOSEBEAK** 148

**CITRUS NIGHTINGOAT** 149

**CITRUS SKUNKLE** 149

# WELCOME TO THE WORLD OF HATCHIMALS:

## HATCHTOPIA™

Can you **imagine** a special place where bluebells ring a happy tune and sunflowers light up the garden? A **hidden land** where an ancient tree giggles, a lake glistens with deep purple waters, and **anything is possible?**

This wonderfully secret world exists! Hatchtopia is home to magical creatures with glittery wings called **Hatchimals**, and you are invited to discover it with them!

10

In this guide, you'll meet all the Season One and Two Hatchimals CollEGGtibles. Learn about their friendly families, magical nests, and sweet personalities to help you get to know your collEGGtion.

And now it's time to take a tour through Hatchtopia and learn all its magical secrets. Use the map on pages 18–19 to begin your journey. Whether you want to have fun in the sun with the Hatchimals of Breezy Beach or to grow new friendships with the Hatchimals of Glittering Garden, this magical world is waiting for you to EGGSplore it!

## GET READY TO HATCH A WHOLE WORLD!

# COllEGGtiNG 101

CollEGGting Hatchimals is fun and easy. There are **hundreds of different creatures** to meet, each with their own distinct personalities and skills.

Have you ever met anything that's **happy-go-lucky** like a penguin and as **quirky and kind** as a koala? That's the friendly Penguala, who is sure to make you smile! What about a creature that's as **brave as an eagle** and as **energetic as a dragon?** The loveable Draggle is as shy as it is curious.

To truly master the art of Hatchimals collEGGting, you'll need to be on the lookout for magical creatures in each of the regions where Hatchimals families live: Savannah, Jungle, Meadow, Farm, Forest, River, Ocean, Desert, and Garden.

But those aren't the only places you'll find Hatchimals. Hatchtopia is full of special hangouts like Season One's Polar Paradise, Lilac Lake, Cloud Cove, Giggle Grove, and Glittering Garden, and Season Two's Snowflake Shire, Magical Meadow, Crystal Canyon, and Citrus Coast.

# HATCHING YOUR COLLEGGtibles

Hatchimals can't hatch without YOU! Rub the heart, and when it changes from purple to pink, that's when you know it's ready to hatch!

Hatchimals CollEGGtibles™ range from common to limited edition in each season!

Season One eggs are purple, while Season Two eggs are pink.

You can tell which season a
Hatchimal is by the base color of the egg,
and which family it's from by the brightly
colored speckles on its shell.

GARDEN

FARM

MEADOW

JUNGLE

FOREST

OCEAN

SAVANNAH

DESERT

RIVER

POLAR PARADISE

LILAC LAKE

GIGGLE GROVE

CLOUD COVE

SNOWFLAKE SHIRE

MAGICAL MEADOW

CRYSTAL CANYON

GLITTERING GARDEN

CITRUS COAST

That way, you can trade eggs with your friends even
before your Hatchimals hatch.

# TRADING TIPS AND TRICKS

You'll have to **search and trade** to complete your collection. Here are some tips and tricks!

Match the speckles to the color of the family in this guide, on the checklist, or on Hatchimals.com/collect.

## ASK YOURSELF:

What color speckles am I looking for? Do I have all the characters I need for that family? If so, trade away!

## DON'T FORGET:

There are Special and Limited Editions in every season. So keep a lookout!

## HERE'S AN EXAMPLE:

If you get a pink egg with red speckles, that means it's from the Farm family in Season Two. If you already have all of the Season Two Farm Hatchimals, go ahead and trade it!

# SEASON TWO MAP OF HATCHTOPIA™
## HATCH A WHOLE WORLD!™

1. Cloud Cove
2. Crystal Canyon
3. Wishing Star Waterfall
4. The Hatchery Nursery
5. Moonlight Mountain
6. Polar Paradise
7. Snowflake Shire
8. Friendship Farm
9. Fabula Forest
10. Lilac Lake
11. Giggle Grove
12. Shimmering Sands
13. Glittering Garden
14. Citrus Coast
15. Magical Meadow
16. Breezy Beach

# GARDEN

All the members of the Garden family are dedicated creatures who truly blossom when they try new things. They believe in planting the seeds of kindness, nurturing their fellow Hatchimals, and **growing** **friendship** all across Hatchtopia. They celebrate the Magnificent Marigolds and Dazzling Daisies that burst through the dirt, spreading sensational scents!

**Planting Day** is the most important day of the year for members of the Garden family. It's a day of new beginnings, promises to loved ones, and dreams for the coming year. Like the flowers that surround them, these Hatchimals are bright and full of life!

# Bunwee
## (ORANGE)

**FUN FACT:**
Orange Bunwee leads the choir and works with its members to create beautiful melodies.

**SEASON:** 1
**RARITY:** Common
**NEST TYPE:** Buttercup
**FLIGHT ABILITY:** 2

**DID YOU KNOW?**
Shining Sunflowers are Orange Bunwee's favorite flower!

## GARDEN

# Bunwee
## (PINK)

**FUN FACT:**
Pink Bunwee is the greeter at the Daisy Schoolhouse and shows new students around.

**SEASON:** 1
**RARITY:** Common
**NEST TYPE:** Buttercup
**FLIGHT ABILITY:** 2

**DID YOU KNOW?**
Pink Bunwee loves Dazzling Daisies!

GARDEN

# MOUSESWIFT (BLUE)

**FUN FACT:**
Blue Mouseswift loves to put on shows for his friends—and they always give a standing ovation!

**SEASON:** 1
**RARITY:** common
**NEST TYPE:** ROSEBUSH
**FLIGHT ABILITY:** 2

**DID YOU KNOW?**
As a born performer, Blue Mouseswift loves it when all eyes are on him!

# MOUSESWIFT (YELLOW)

**FUN FACT:**
Yellow Mouseswift is a bookworm who loves getting lost in a good story.

**SEASON:** 1
**RARITY:** common
**NEST TYPE:** ROSEBUSH
**FLIGHT ABILITY:** 3

**DID YOU KNOW?**
Yellow Mouseswift has read more books than any other Hatchimal!

# SNAILTAIL
## (GREEN)

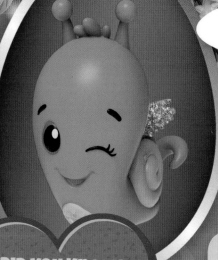

### FUN FACT:
Green Snailtail sometimes gets lost in his own imagination rather than focusing on the task at hand.

**DID YOU KNOW?**
Green Snailtail loves to make dreamcatchers!

**SEASON:** 1
**RARITY:** RARE
**NEST TYPE:** EIGHTLIP
**FLIGHT ABILITY:** 3

# SNAILTAIL
## (YELLOW)

### FUN FACT:
Yellow Snailtail is a creative creature who loves capturing the beauty of Hatchtopia in her own style.

**SEASON:** 1
**RARITY:** ULTRA RARE
**NEST TYPE:** EIGHTLIP
**FLIGHT ABILITY:** 4

**DID YOU KNOW?**
Yellow Snailtail painted a mural that shows all of Hatchtopia!

GARDEN

# BEEBULL
## (PINK)

### DID YOU KNOW?
Pink Beebull has a sweet tooth!

**SEASON:** 2
**RARITY:** common
**NEST TYPE:** BUTTERCUP
**FLIGHT ABILITY:** 4

### FUN FACT:
Pink Beebull is a sweet thing who makes Hatchy Honey for tea party days . . . and every other day, too!

# BEEBULL
## (YELLOW)

### FUN FACT:
Yellow Beebull always watches over her friends—she hates to see anyone get hurt!

### DID YOU KNOW?
She takes extra care of new eggs before they hatch!

**SEASON:** 2
**RARITY:** common
**NEST TYPE:** BUTTERCUP
**FLIGHT ABILITY:** 4

# BUNWEE
## (YELLOW)

**FUN FACT:**
Yellow Bunwee is always studying and gets the best grades at school!

**DID YOU KNOW?**
Yellow Bunwee is always jumping for joy!

**SEASON:** 2
**RARITY:** COMMON
**NEST TYPE:** ROSEBUSH
**FLIGHT ABILITY:** 4

# BUTTERPUFF
## (PEACH)

**FUN FACT:**
Peach Butterpuff loves making new friends!

**DID YOU KNOW?**
HFF stands for Hatch Friends Forever!

**SEASON:** 2
**RARITY:** RARE
**NEST TYPE:** EIGHTLIP
**FLIGHT ABILITY:** 5

GARDEN

## BUTTERPUFF
### (PINK)

### FUN FACT:
Pink Butterpuff is a storyteller EGGStraordinaire! She loves to gather her friends around and tell them dramatic stories that she can't help acting out.

**SEASON:** 2
**RARITY:** Common
**NEST TYPE:** EIGHTLIP
**FLIGHT ABILITY:** 5

### DID YOU KNOW?
Pink Butterpuff dreams of writing a book of her favorite stories!

## DRAGONFLIP
### (BLUE)

### FUN FACT:
Blue Dragonflip always finds out any news first and loves to share it.

### DID YOU KNOW?
She makes the morning announcements at the Daisy Schoolhouse!

**SEASON:** 2
**RARITY:** Common
**NEST TYPE:** EIGHTLIP
**FLIGHT ABILITY:** 5

# DRAGONFLIP
## (PURPLE)

**FUN FACT:**
Purple Dragonflip has an eye for detail, and paints beautiful portraits of all her friends.

**DID YOU KNOW?**
Purple Dragonflip paints with Willow Wood brushes!

**SEASON:** 2
**RARITY:** RARE
**NEST TYPE:** EIGHTLIP
**FLIGHT ABILITY:** 5

GARDEN

# FROWL
## (BLUE)

**FUN FACT:**
Blue Frowl knows it's important to lend a helping hand. He's always ready to go the EGGStra mile for anyone who needs him.

**DID YOU KNOW?**
Blue Frowl is hypnotized by Hatchtopia history!

**SEASON:** 2
**RARITY:** ULTRA RARE
**NEST TYPE:** ROSEBUSH
**FLIGHT ABILITY:** 3

GARDEN

# FROWL
## (GREEN)

### FUN FACT:
Green Frowl uses his quick tongue to catch bugs and to tidy up around the garden. He likes to keep the world clean!

**SEASON:** 2
**RARITY:** RARE
**NEST TYPE:** ROSEBUSH
**FLIGHT ABILITY:** 3

### DID YOU KNOW?
Green Frowl decorates his to-do lists and checks off with stickers and glitter!

# MOUSESWIFT
## (MAGENTA)

### FUN FACT:
Magenta Mouseswift has a great imagination and loves acting out stories with her friends.

### DID YOU KNOW?
Magenta Mouseswift gives her friends the silliest nicknames!

**SEASON:** 2
**RARITY:** COMMON
**NEST TYPE:** ROSEBUSH
**FLIGHT ABILITY:** 3

# FARM

Farm Hatchimals are hard workers who also love to have fun. Whether they're frolicking through the Shining Sunflowers or hopping in the Honey Hay, this pleasant pasture is the perfect place for them.

Plus, members of the Farm family know that **big responsibilities come with big rewards.** Putting in the work to grow fresh veggies and juicy fruits means big Farm family dinners filled with tasty treats. And after a harvest feast, there's nothing better than letting loose in the Hay Barn, where everyone gathers before heading to their nests to rest.

# LAMBLET
## (BLUE)

**FUN FACT:**
Blue Lamblet likes to dig in the dirt—and roll around in it!

**DID YOU KNOW?**
Blue Lamblet's prized possession is his rock collEGGtion!

**SEASON:** 1
**RARITY:** ULTRA RARE
**NEST TYPE:** SUNFLOWER
**FLIGHT ABILITY:** 4

# LAMBLET
## (PINK)

**FUN FACT:**
Pink Lamblet loves to share her fruits and veggies with all her friends!

**DID YOU KNOW?**
Pink Lamblet's favorite vegetable is the Rhooby Radish!

**SEASON:** 1
**RARITY:** COMMON
**NEST TYPE:** SUNFLOWER
**FLIGHT ABILITY:** 3

# PIGPIPER
## (PINK)

**FUN FACT:**
Pink Pigpiper loves to snuggle. Group hugs are her favorite!

**SEASON: 1**
**RARITY: Common**
**NEST TYPE: ABUNDANT VEGGIE**
**FLIGHT ABILITY: 3**

**DID YOU KNOW?**
Pink Pigpiper loves to vacation at Shimmering Sands!

# PIGPIPER
## (YELLOW)

**FUN FACT:**
Yellow Pigpiper takes things slow. He's all about thinking something through before diving into action.

**DID YOU KNOW?**
Yellow Pigpiper frequently naps through lunch!

**SEASON: 1**
**RARITY: RARE**
**NEST TYPE: ABUNDANT VEGGIE**
**FLIGHT ABILITY: 3**

# PONETTE
## (ORANGE)

**FUN FACT:**
Orange Ponette loves learning from the past. He's an EGGSpert in Hatchtopian history!

**DID YOU KNOW?**
Orange Ponette enjoys books with true stories!

**SEASON:** 1
**RARITY:** Common
**NEST TYPE:** Honey Hay
**FLIGHT ABILITY:** 3

# PONETTE
## (PINK)

**FUN FACT:**
Pink Ponette likes to put everything in its place. She's in charge of keeping the barn tools in order.

**DID YOU KNOW?**
Pink Ponette loves to make Honey Hay hammocks!

**SEASON:** 1
**RARITY:** Common
**NEST TYPE:** Honey Hay
**FLIGHT ABILITY:** 3

FARM

# CHICKCHAFF (ORANGE)

**FUN FACT:**

Orange Chickchaff loves to make her home look pretty. She fills it with beautiful origami creations!

**SeASON:** 2
**RARITY:** common
**NEST TYPE:** Honey Hay
**FLIGHT ABILITY:** 3

**DID YOU KNOW?**

Orange Chickchaff loves heading down to Breezy Beach to collect seashells!

# CHICKCHAFF (RED)

**FUN FACT:**

Red Chickchaff makes yummy desserts with the fruits from the farm!

**DID YOU KNOW?**

Red Chickchaff runs a fun food festival!

**SeASON:** 2
**RARITY:** RARE
**NEST TYPE:** Honey Hay
**FLIGHT ABILITY:** 4

# DONKEMU
## (BLUE)

**FUN FACT:**
Blue Donkemu loves to play party games, but never try to pin a tail on him!

**DID YOU KNOW?**
Blue Donkemu has a laugh everyone loves!

**SEASON:** 2
**RARITY:** COMMON
**NEST TYPE:** ABUNDANT VEGGIE
**FLIGHT ABILITY:** 3

FARM

# DONKEMU
## (PINK)

**FUN FACT:**
Pink Donkemu is always thinking of others. She throws all her friends' special Hatchy Birthday parties.

**DID YOU KNOW?**
Pink Donkemu likes to hang out at Wishing Star Waterfall!

**SEASON:** 2
**RARITY:** COMMON
**NEST TYPE:** SUNFLOWER
**FLIGHT ABILITY:** 2

# LLAMALOON
## (PINK)

**FUN FACT:**
Pink Llamaloon is philosophical. She's always wondering what came first: the Hatchimal or the egg.

**SEASON: 2**
**RARITY: RARE**
**NEST TYPE: SUNFLOWER**
**FLIGHT ABILITY: 4**

**DID YOU KNOW?**
Pink Llamaloon is always reading!

# LLAMALOON
## (PURPLE)

**FUN FACT:**
Purple Llamaloon takes karate classes every week!

**DID YOU KNOW?**
Purple Llamaloon is the safety monitor at school!

**SEASON: 2**
**RARITY: RARE**
**NEST TYPE: SUNFLOWER**
**FLIGHT ABILITY: 3**

# MACOW
## (ORANGE)

**FUN FACT:**
Orange Macow loves a sweet celebration. She bakes amazing cakes for her friends' Hatchy Birthday parties.

**DID YOU KNOW?**
Orange Macow has a colorful cake-making kit!

**SEASON:** 2
**RARITY:** common
**NEST TYPE:** ABUNDANT VEGGIE
**FLIGHT ABILITY:** 3

FARM

# MACOW
## (WHITE)

**FUN FACT:**
White Macow always has a cool new look to show off. She is the stylish friend of the pack!

**DID YOU KNOW?**
White Macow likes to dance to rock moo-sic!

**SEASON:** 2
**RARITY:** common
**NEST TYPE:** ABUNDANT VEGGIE
**FLIGHT ABILITY:** 2

# NIGHTINGOAT
## (Blue)

### FUN FACT:
Blue Nightingoat is a hard worker who likes to do a good job at anything he takes on. He's the best corn husker on the farm.

**SEASON:** 2
**RARITY:** ULTRA RARE
**NEST TYPE:** HONEY HAY
**FLIGHT ABILITY:** 3

### DID YOU KNOW?
Blue Nightingoat always lends a helping horn!

# NIGHTINGOAT
## (TEAL)

### FUN FACT:
Teal Nightingoat is ultra friendly and knows everyone. She's never afraid to introduce herself and make a new friend!

### DID YOU KNOW?
Teal Nightingoat likes playing games that bring everyone together!

**SEASON:** 2
**RARITY:** COMMON
**NEST TYPE:** HONEY HAY
**FLIGHT ABILITY:** 2

# Ponette
## (TEAL)

**FUN FACT:**
Teal Ponette loves to make her friends feel special. She makes beautiful friendship bracelets.

**DID YOU KNOW?**
Teal Ponette often breaks into song!

**Season:** 2
**RARITY:** common
**NEST TYPE:** ABUNDANT VEGGIE
**FLIGHT ABILITY:** 4

# Ponette
## (BLUE)

**FUN FACT:**
Blue Ponette always looks on the bright side of things, no matter the situation!

**DID YOU KNOW?**
Blue Ponette dislikes neigh-sayers!

**Season:** 2
**RARITY:** common
**NEST TYPE:** SUNFLOWER
**FLIGHT ABILITY:** 5

PARTY Time

# MEADOW

Meadow Hatchimals love the springtime. That's when the breeze flutters freely and the sun on the meadow sparkles with a thousand dewdrops. Sweet-smelling flowers dot the greenest grass in all of Hatchtopia.

The Hatchimals of the Meadow family are **the most thoughtful creatures around.** Whether they are organizing a game of Hatchy Ball, turning cartwheels through the tall grass, or weaving Dazzling Daisy chains, they are always sure to **make their friends feel included.**

# HEDGYHEN
## (GREEN)

**FUN FACT:**

Green Hedgyhen leads the nature club on field trips.

**SEASON:** 1
**RARITY:** RARE
**NEST TYPE:** LULLABY GRASS
**FLIGHT ABILITY:** 1

**DID YOU KNOW?**
Green Hedgyhen loves hiking up the icy mountains of Polar Paradise!

# HEDGYHEN
## (PINK)

**FUN FACT:**

Pink Hedgyhen runs the Hatchtopia book club which meets every month.

**DID YOU KNOW?**
Pink Hedgyhen helps younger Hatchimals learn to read!

**SEASON:** 1
**RARITY:** RARE
**NEST TYPE:** LULLABY GRASS
**FLIGHT ABILITY:** 3

# KITTYCAN
## (BLUE)

**FUN FACT:**
Blue Kittycan sings in a glee club with her friends.

**DID YOU KNOW?**
Blue Kittycan has purr-fect pitch!

**SEASON:** 1
**RARITY:** common
**NEST TYPE:** EUCALYPTUS TREE
**FLIGHT ABILITY:** 2

**MEADOW**

# KITTYCAN
## (YELLOW)

**FUN FACT:**
Yellow Kittycan loves to race through meadows, climb up mountains, and sail the high seas.

**DID YOU KNOW?**
Yellow Kittycan loves to compete in the Hatchy Games!

**SEASON:** 1
**RARITY:** common
**NEST TYPE:** EUCALYPTUS TREE
**FLIGHT ABILITY:** 2

43

MEADOW

# PUPPIT
# (BLUE)

### FUN FACT:
Blue Puppit doesn't mind getting his paws dirty—he'll work to achieve his dreams!

**SEASON:** 1
**RARITY:** ULTRA RARE
**NEST TYPE:** LULLABY GRASS
**FLIGHT ABILITY:** 4

### DID YOU KNOW?
Blue Puppit loves digging for treasure!

# PUPPIT
# (PURPLE)

### FUN FACT:
All the Hatchimals love silly Purple Puppit because he can always make them laugh!

### DID YOU KNOW?
Purple Puppit is known for doggie-paddling in Lilac Lake!

**SEASON:** 1
**RARITY:** COMMON
**NEST TYPE:** LULLABY GRASS
**FLIGHT ABILITY:** 5

# PLEASANT PASTURES

# JUNGLE

The wild and wonderful Hatchimals of the Jungle family enjoy hot days and balmy nights. With plenty of Palm Leaves, Orange Ferns, and Daffodil Trees, the air always smells sweet and fresh.

All Jungle Hatchimals are feisty and free, passionate and persistent. They know every corner of the jungle. This means they can swing from vine to vine to get around quickly, and hide in the shade of the jungle's canopy. They find the best spots to lounge in a hammock and enjoy the tropical breeze.

The Jungle Hatchimals all have the **adventure bug.** It's an itch that can only be scratched by setting out on a quest. Sometimes that means climbing to the top of the coldest peak in Polar Paradise, while other times it means diving to the bottom of the sea at Breezy Beach. These Hatchimals **push themselves to EGGStremes** and have lots of fun doing it!

# MONKIWI
## (BLUE)

### FUN FACT:
Blue Monkiwi is one of a kind. He marches to the beat of his own drum.

**DID YOU KNOW?**
Blue Monkiwi likes to color outside the lines!

**SEASON:** 1
**RARITY:** ULTRA RARE
**NEST TYPE:** PALM LEAF
**FLIGHT ABILITY:** 4

**JUNGLE**

# MONKIWI
## (PINK)

### FUN FACT:
Pink Monkiwi loves to swing from tree to tree!

**DID YOU KNOW?**
Pink Monkiwi dreams of being an acrobat!

**SEASON:** 1
**RARITY:** common
**NEST TYPE:** PALM LEAF
**FLIGHT ABILITY:** 2

JUNGLE

# PANDOR
## (BLUE)

## FUN FACT:
Blue Pandor makes up dance moves to teach her friends.

**SEASON:** 1
**RARITY:** RARE
**NEST TYPE:** DAFFODIL TREE
**FLIGHT ABILITY:** 4

### DID YOU KNOW?
Blue Pandor loves going to the ballet!

# PANDOR
## (PURPLE)

## FUN FACT:
Purple Pandor is kind and considerate. She always sends get-well cards when her friends are under the weather.

### DID YOU KNOW?
Purple Pandor volunteers in her free time!

**SEASON:** 1
**RARITY:** RARE
**NEST TYPE:** DAFFODIL TREE
**FLIGHT ABILITY:** 3

# TIGRETTE
## (BLUE)

### FUN FACT:
Blue Tigrette can't stop moving. He's the star player on the Hatchimals baskEGGball team.

### DID YOU KNOW?
Blue Tigrette is a break-dancing machine!

**SEASON:** 1
**RARITY:** Common
**NEST TYPE:** ORANGE FERNS
**FLIGHT ABILITY:** 2

# TIGRETTE
## (ORANGE)

### FUN FACT:
Orange Tigrette considers himself the leader of the group. He likes to do things his own way!

### DID YOU KNOW?
Orange Tigrette is brave, but also a big softy!

**SEASON:** 1
**RARITY:** Common
**NEST TYPE:** ORANGE FERNS
**FLIGHT ABILITY:** 3

JUNGLE

# ALBASLOTH
## (PURPLE)

**FUN FACT:**
Purple Albasloth has the prettiest singing voice around.

**SEASON:** 2
**RARITY:** RARE
**NEST TYPE:** PALM LEAF
**FLIGHT ABILITY:** 1

**DID YOU KNOW?**
Purple Albasloth enjoys sing-alongs!

# ALBASLOTH
## (PINK)

**FUN FACT:**
Pink Albasloth has a quick mind. She can come up with a solution to any problem!

**DID YOU KNOW?**
Pink Albasloth relaxes with a challenging crossword puzzle!

**SEASON:** 2
**RARITY:** RARE
**NEST TYPE:** PALM LEAF
**FLIGHT ABILITY:** 1

# ANTEAGLE
## (PINK)

### FUN FACT:
Pink Anteagle would rather catch up with friends than do anything else!

### DID YOU KNOW?
Pink Anteagle enjoys having deep conversations—while flying through the air!

**SEASON:** 2
**RARITY:** RARE
**NEST TYPE:** DAFFODIL TREE
**FLIGHT ABILITY:** 5

JUNGLE

# ANTEAGLE
## (PURPLE)

### FUN FACT:
Purple Anteagle has traveled to every corner of Hatchtopia, and always brings back souvenirs for her friends!

### DID YOU KNOW?
Purple Anteagle never stays in one spot for long!

**SEASON:** 2
**RARITY:** COMMON
**NEST TYPE:** DAFFODIL TREE
**FLIGHT ABILITY:** 5

JUNGLE

# CHAMELOON
## (BLUE)

**FUN FACT:**
Blue Chameloon loves to be bold. Her love of bright colors keeps her from blending in!

**SEASON:** 2
**RARITY:** Common
**NEST TYPE:** PALM LEAF
**FLIGHT ABILITY:** 3

**DID YOU KNOW?**
Blue Chameloon can shop till she drops!

# CHAMELOON
## (YELLOW)

**FUN FACT:**
Yellow Chameloon can be shy at times, until she gets to know others! Only then does she let her sweet, funny self show.

**DID YOU KNOW?**
Yellow Chameloon keeps a journal!

**SEASON:** 2
**RARITY:** Common
**NEST TYPE:** PALM LEAF
**FLIGHT ABILITY:** 2

# GORILLABEE
## (BLUE)

### FUN FACT:
Blue Gorillabee is very flexible. She knows how to go with the flow!

### DID YOU KNOW?
Blue Gorillabee practices yoga every day!

**SEASON:** 2
**RARITY:** ULTRA RARE
**NEST TYPE:** ORANGE FERNS
**FLIGHT ABILITY:** 2

# GORILLABEE
## (PURPLE)

JUNGLE

### FUN FACT:
Purple Gorillabee always has a swing in her step and a song in her heart. In fact, she doesn't speak, she only sings!

### DID YOU KNOW?
Purple Gorillabee's hobby is ballroom dancing!

**SEASON:** 2
**RARITY:** Common
**NEST TYPE:** ORANGE FERNS
**FLIGHT ABILITY:** 3

JUNGLE

# PANDOR
## (TEAL)

**FUN FACT:**
Teal Pandor has a never-ending supply of kindness—and isn't afraid to use it!

**SEASON:** 2
**RARITY:** COMMON
**NEST TYPE:** ORANGE FERNS
**FLIGHT ABILITY:** 4

**DID YOU KNOW?**
Teal Pandor's favorite place to hang out is Citrus Coast!

# PARROO
## (RED)

**FUN FACT:**
Red Parroo is a chatterbox with a kind word for everyone.

**SEASON:** 2*
**RARITY:** COMMON
**NEST TYPE:** DAFFODIL TREE
**FLIGHT ABILITY:** 4

**DID YOU KNOW?**
Red Parroo's motto is 'Time flies when you're talking with friends!'

*Exclusive to Season 2 playset

# TIGRETTE
## (PINK)

### FUN FACT:
Pink Tigrette likes the thrill of a little danger. She's willing to take some risks to have a good time!

### DID YOU KNOW?
Pink Tigrette likes watching scary movies!

**SEASON:** 2
**RARITY:** common
**NEST TYPE:** ORANGE FERNS
**FLIGHT ABILITY:** 4

# TOUCOO
## (BLUE)

### FUN FACT:
Blue Toucoo loves to cook because she loves to eat. She collects exotic ingredients to use in fancy meals for her friends. Bon appétit!

### DID YOU KNOW?
Blue Toucoo is writing a cookbook!

**SEASON:** 2
**RARITY:** common
**NEST TYPE:** DAFFODIL TREE
**FLIGHT ABILITY:** 5

JUNGLE

55

JUNGLE

# TOUCOO
## (PINK)

**FUN FACT:**
Pink Toucoo is a builder with an eye for beauty. She constructs beautiful nests for the other Hatchimals.

**SEASON:** 2
**RARITY:** Common
**NEST TYPE:** DAFFODIL TREE
**FLIGHT ABILITY:** 5

**DID YOU KNOW?**
Pink Toucoo has plans for the ultimate sand castle!

# BEST BUDS

# FOREST

Forest Hatchimals enjoy flitting through the towering Orchid Pine trees and collEGGting colorful leaves that fall from the Lovely Lavender Oaks. Whether they are setting records, setting the style, or setting a good example, the Hatchimals of the Forest family are **known for being leaders.** These trendsetters follow their passions to scale the tallest tree and cross the widest stream, and their friends can't help but follow along. The Forest Hatchimals are always **forging new paths!**

But always taking the lead can be pretty tiring. Luckily, the Forest family Hatchimals are **EGGSpert nesters.** They build the snuggliest beds in Hatchtopia, high up in the treetops. So after a long day at the front of the pack, they can cuddle up in comfort and rest for whatever tomorrow may bring!

# CHIPADEE
## (ORANGE)

**FUN FACT:**
Orange Chipadee loves meeting new Hatchimals and making new friends!

**DID YOU KNOW?**
Orange Chipadee makes welcome baskets for new Hatchimals!

**SEASON:** 1
**RARITY:** common
**NEST TYPE:** ORCHID PINE
**FLIGHT ABILITY:** 5

**FOREST**

# CHIPADEE
## (PINK)

**FUN FACT:**
Pink Chipadee has the special skill of conducting the musical trees of Fabula Forest!

**SEASON:** 1
**RARITY:** ULTRA RARE
**NEST TYPE:** ORCHID PINE
**FLIGHT ABILITY:** 4

**DID YOU KNOW?**
Pink Chipadee used the Weeping Willow tree to make her conductor's baton!

# DEERALOO
## (BLUE)

### FUN FACT:

Blue Deeraloo goes on a long walk through Fabula Forest every day to feel at one with her world.

**SEASON:** 1
**RARITY:** Common
**NEST TYPE:** PINK MAPLE
**FLIGHT ABILITY:** 4

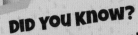

### DID YOU KNOW?

The forest trees play their own music! Blue Deeraloo loves to skip to their beat!

# DEERALOO
## (PINK)

### FUN FACT:

Pink Deeraloo loves to solve riddles. She also writes the crossword puzzle in the Hatchy Gazette.

### DID YOU KNOW?

Pink Deeraloo is a trivia champion!

**SEASON:** 1
**RARITY:** Common
**NEST TYPE:** PINK MAPLE
**FLIGHT ABILITY:** 4

**FOREST**

# RASPOON
## (BLUE)

**FUN FACT:**
Blue Raspoon is very thoughtful. She thinks about both sides of a situation before making a decision.

**DID YOU KNOW?**
Hatchimals come from far and wide for her thoughtful advice!

**SEASON:** 1
**RARITY:** RARE
**NEST TYPE:** LAVENDER OAK
**FLIGHT ABILITY:** 2

# RASPOON
## (PURPLE)

**FUN FACT:**
Purple Raspoon is curious and playful and loves living in the forest!

**DID YOU KNOW?**
Purple Raspoon is the Hatch-and-Seek champion!

**SEASON:** 1
**RARITY:** COMMON
**NEST TYPE:** LAVENDER OAK
**FLIGHT ABILITY:** 2

# SKUNKLe
## (GReeN)

**FUN FACT:**
Green Skunkle loves to organize fabulous dance parties!

**SEASON: 1**
**RARITY: RARe**
**NEST TYPE: LAVeNDeR OAK**
**FLIGHT ABILITY: 3**

**DID YOU KNOW?**
Green Skunkle is great at Fly-Dancing! That's when you fly and dance at the same time!

# SKUNKLe
## (PURPLe)

**FUN FACT:**
Purple Skunkle is an award-winning photographer, but she would never brag about it.

**DID YOU KNOW?**
Purple Skunkle owns fifteen different cameras!

**SEASON: 1**
**RARITY: Common**
**NEST TYPE: LAVeNDeR OAK**
**FLIGHT ABILITY: 2**

# DEERALOO
## (MAGENTA)

### FUN FACT:
Magenta Deeraloo is energetic and excited about every opportunity for adventure that comes her way!

### DID YOU KNOW?
Magenta Deeraloo loves to spend time in the library!

**SEASON:** 2
**RARITY:** COMMON
**NEST TYPE:** ORCHID PINE
**FLIGHT ABILITY:** 3

# FOXFIN
## (PURPLE)

### FUN FACT:
Purple Foxfin is super crafty! She loves making adorable hats and accessories for all of her friends!

### DID YOU KNOW?
Purple Foxfin loves EGGSploring the forest for new materials to use!

**SEASON:** 2
**RARITY:** ULTRA RARE
**NEST TYPE:** ORCHID PINE
**FLIGHT ABILITY:** 3

FOREST

## FOXFIN
### (RED)

**FUN FACT:**
Red Foxfin is full of fun facts about Hatchtopia, and she loves to share them with anyone who will listen!

**SEASON:** 2
**RARITY:** Common
**NEST TYPE:** ORCHID PINE
**FLIGHT ABILITY:** 3

**DID YOU KNOW?**
Red Foxfin's goal is to visit every place in Hatchtopia!

## HUMMINGBEAR
### (PINK)

**FUN FACT:**
Pink Hummingbear is one of Hatchtopia's favorite teachers at the Daisy Schoolhouse!

**DID YOU KNOW?**
Her favorite subject is GeEGGraphy!

**SEASON:** 2
**RARITY:** RARE
**NEST TYPE:** PINK MAPLE
**FLIGHT ABILITY:** 1

# HUMMINGBEAR
## (PURPLE)

**FUN FACT:**
Purple Hummingbear has so much love to share. She can't help giving a hug to all the Hatchimals she meets!

**DID YOU KNOW?**
Her favorite type of hug is the bear hug.

**SEASON:** 2
**RARITY:** common
**NEST TYPE:** PINK MAPLE
**FLIGHT ABILITY:** 4

# MOOSEBEAK
## (BLUE)

**FUN FACT:**
Blue Moosebeak is not exactly graceful. He can't help bumping into trees, shrubs, and his friends . . . but he always says he's sorry!

**SEASON:** 2
**RARITY:** RARE
**NEST TYPE:** ORCHID PINE
**FLIGHT ABILITY:** 2

**DID YOU KNOW?**
His goal is to become a great flyer and make it to Cloud Cove!

FOREST

# MOOSEBEAK
## (PURPLE)

**FUN FACT:**
Purple Moosebeak believes good manners are always in style and never forgets to say please and thank you.

**SEASON:** 2
**RARITY:** COMMON
**NEST TYPE:** ORCHID PINE
**FLIGHT ABILITY:** 4

**DID YOU KNOW?**
Purple Moosebeak and Purple Hummingbear are HFFs!

# OWLING
## (PINK)

**FUN FACT:**
Pink Owling is the most sophisticated of the Hatchimals. She loves an afternoon tea party or a night at the opera.

**DID YOU KNOW?**
Pink Owling keeps track of hoo's hoo in Hatchtopia!

**SEASON:** 2
**RARITY:** ULTRA RARE
**NEST TYPE:** LAVENDER OAK
**FLIGHT ABILITY:** 5

# OWLING
## (TEAL)

**FUN FACT:**
Teal Owling thinks creatively. If a tough problem is at hand, she'll find new ways to solve it.

**DID YOU KNOW?**
Teal Owling is as funny as she is wise— friends say she's a hoot!

**SEASON:** 2
**RARITY:** Common
**NEST TYPE:** LAVENDER OAK
**FLIGHT ABILITY:** 5

**FOREST**

# POSSWIFT
## (MAGENTA)

**FUN FACT:**
Magenta Posswift loves to EGGSplore Hatchtopia on her own. She knows she has friends wherever she goes!

**SEASON:** 2
**RARITY:** RARE
**NEST TYPE:** LAVENDER OAK
**FLIGHT ABILITY:** 2

**DID YOU KNOW?**
Magenta Posswift writes a blog so her friends can keep up with her adventures!

# POSSWIFT
## (PURPLE)

**FUN FACT:**
Purple Posswift is a total fashionista. She has great taste that keeps her flying in style.

**SEASON:** 2
**RARITY:** common
**NEST TYPE:** LAVENDER OAK
**FLIGHT ABILITY:** 2

**DID YOU KNOW?**
Purple Posswift's chic style is influenced by her natural surroundings!

# RASPOON
## (TEAL)

**FUN FACT:**
Teal Raspoon loves to run fast—especially during the annual Hatchy Race!

**SEASON:** 2
**RARITY:** common
**NEST TYPE:** ORCHID PINE
**FLIGHT ABILITY:** 2

**DID YOU KNOW?**
Teal Raspoon has over fifty medals!

FOREST FRIENDS

# OCEAN

Cozy Coral that shines through the clear blue water and bright, sparkling sand make Ocean Hatchimals feel right at home. Fun-loving and free, the members of the Ocean family are **playful pals** who enjoy every activity Breezy Beach has to offer and are always up for a game. But they also remember to **breathe the fresh ocean air** and let it give them a sense of peace.

All the members of the Ocean family have a special skill in common: **they are all EGGStraordinary swimmers.** That's right—they can fly <u>and</u> swim, since they hatch underwater. The Ocean family Hatchimals are the perfect partners when you feel like **diving into adventure!**

# DOLFINCH
## (BLUE)

### FUN FACT:
Blue Dolfinch makes seashell crowns for new Hatchimals!

### DID YOU KNOW?
Blue Dolfinch loves to help the Ocean Hatchimals hatch!

**SEASON:** 1
**RARITY:** common
**NEST TYPE:** BLISS BUBBLE
**FLIGHT ABILITY:** 1

**OCEAN**

# DOLFINCH
## (PINK)

### FUN FACT:
Pink Dolfinch prefers the simple things in life. Her favorite activity is relaxing!

### DID YOU KNOW?
Bliss Bubbles allow you to breathe underwater!

**SEASON:** 1
**RARITY:** common
**NEST TYPE:** BLISS BUBBLE
**FLIGHT ABILITY:** 1

OCEAN

# CRABLER
## (RED)

**FUN FACT:**
Red Crabler has the tidiest nest and is always cleaning up after others, keeping the beach clean for everyone.

**SEASON:** 2
**RARITY:** common
**NEST TYPE:** SPARKLING SAND
**FLIGHT ABILITY:** 2

**DID YOU KNOW?**
Red Crabler loves to reuse the items he collects to build new things!

# CRABLER
## (YELLOW)

**FUN FACT:**
Yellow Crabler is quite the designer. She builds the biggest and most amazing sand castles at Breezy Beach!

**DID YOU KNOW?**
She wins the sand-castle contest every year at the Hatchy Games!

**SEASON:** 2
**RARITY:** common
**NEST TYPE:** SPARKLING SAND
**FLIGHT ABILITY:** 3

# DOLFINCH
## (TEAL)

**FUN FACT:**
Teal Dolfinch teaches swimming lessons at Breezy Beach and is always in a happy mood!

**DID YOU KNOW?**
Most baby Hatchimals know how to fly, but they need help learning to swim!

**SEASON:** 2
**RARITY:** Common
**NEST TYPE:** BLISS BUBBLE
**FLIGHT ABILITY:** 2

**OCEAN**

# OCTAPITTA
## (BLUE)

**FUN FACT:**
Blue Octapitta is a great worker who uses her eight magical arms to do lots of things at the same time.

**SEASON:** 2
**RARITY:** Common
**NEST TYPE:** COZY CORAL
**FLIGHT ABILITY:** 1

**DID YOU KNOW?**
Blue Octapitta is the best long-distance swimmer in Hatchtopia!

OCEAN

# OCTAPITTA
## (PINK)

### FUN FACT:
Pink Octapitta has arms made for drumming. She makes great beats and can play the drums like no other!

**SEASON:** 2
**RARITY:** RARE
**NEST TYPE:** COZY CORAL
**FLIGHT ABILITY:** 2

### DID YOU KNOW?
Pink Octapitta plays eight instruments in her one-man band!

# PENGUALA
## (MAGENTA)

### FUN FACT:
Magenta Penguala isn't afraid of taking risks. He loves to surf the giant waves at Breezy Beach.

### DID YOU KNOW?
Magenta Penguala penned the term Hatch-Ten!

**SEASON:** 2
**RARITY:** COMMON
**NEST TYPE:** SPARKLING SAND
**FLIGHT ABILITY:** 4

# SEASPOON
## (BLUE)

### FUN FACT:
Blue Seaspoon is part seahorse! No wonder she spends most of her time underwater!

### DID YOU KNOW?
She has the largest collEGGtion of seashells and sea gems in Hatchtopia!

**SEASON:** 2
**RARITY:** common
**NEST TYPE:** BLISS BUBBLE
**FLIGHT ABILITY:** 3

OCEAN

# SEASPOON
## (PINK)

### FUN FACT:
Pink Seaspoon grabs the attention of everyone around her with a special magic that's all her own.

### DID YOU KNOW?
She specializes in synchronized swimming!

**SEASON:** 2
**RARITY:** ULTRA RARE
**NEST TYPE:** BLISS BUBBLE
**FLIGHT ABILITY:** 5

# HOT HANGOUTS

# SAVANNAH

Savannah Hatchimals are happiest when they're tumbling through the Glowing Grass of this hot, dry land. The members of the Savannah family are **well-seasoned travelers who love to EGGSplore.** They are bold seekers who yearn to learn, and live for new discoveries. Their questing natures can make them restless at times, but they're always happy to return home to their friends!

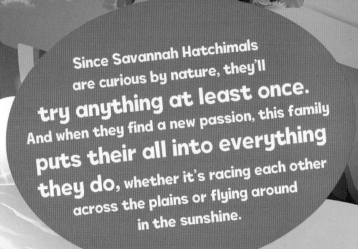

Since Savannah Hatchimals are curious by nature, they'll **try anything at least once.** And when they find a new passion, this family **puts their all into everything they do,** whether it's racing each other across the plains or flying around in the sunshine.

SAVANNAH

# ELEFLY
## (BLUE)

**FUN FACT:**
Blue Elefly daydreams about faraway places, then pores over travel guides to make her dreams come true.

**SEASON:** 1
**RARITY:** COMMON
**NEST TYPE:** GLOWING GRASS
**FLIGHT ABILITY:** 2

**DID YOU KNOW?**
Blue Elefly's favorite place to EGGSplore is Crystal Canyon!

# ELEFLY
## (GREEN)

**FUN FACT:**
Green Elefly has the heart and soul of a poet. He likes to serenade his friends with a different sparkling poem each day.

**DID YOU KNOW?**
Green Elefly composes special birthday songs for everyone he knows!

**SEASON:** 1
**RARITY:** RARE
**NEST TYPE:** GLOWING GRASS
**FLIGHT ABILITY:** 3

# GIRREO
## (PINK)

**FUN FACT:**
Pink Girreo likes going on adventures with friends, and she always makes sure they get home safely.

**DID YOU KNOW?**
Pink Girreo loves to invite new Hatchimals on her journeys!

**SEASON:** 1
**RARITY:** common
**NEST TYPE:** SPARKLING SAND
**FLIGHT ABILITY:** 2

**SAVANNAH**

# GIRREO
## (YELLOW)

**FUN FACT:**
Yellow Girreo is one of the best flyers in Savannah!

**DID YOU KNOW?**
Her long neck allows her to do cool tricks in the air!

**SEASON:** 1
**RARITY:** ULTRA RARE
**NEST TYPE:** SPARKLING SAND
**FLIGHT ABILITY:** 4

SAVANNAH

# LEORIOLE (ORANGE)

**FUN FACT:**
Orange Leoriole can't be tamed. He's got a rebellious streak, but he's really a purr-fect gentleman inside.

**SEASON: 1**
**RARITY: RARE**
**NEST TYPE: DESERT FLOWER**
**FLIGHT ABILITY: 5**

**DID YOU KNOW?**
Orange Leoriole can always claw his way out of a tight spot!

# LEORIOLE (PINK)

**FUN FACT:**
Pink Leoriole loves giving tours of Savannah to new Hatchimals!

**DID YOU KNOW?**
Pink Leoriole can roar loud enough to make the tumbleweeds roll!

**SEASON: 1**
**RARITY: COMMON**
**NEST TYPE: DESERT FLOWER**
**FLIGHT ABILITY: 2**

# ZEBRUSH
## (PINK)

**FUN FACT:**
Pink Zebrush is one of the sassiest and most fashionable Hatchimals around!

**DID YOU KNOW?**
Pink Zebrush is part of Team Hatch—helping hard-to-hatch eggs come to life!

**SEASON:** 1
**RARITY:** Common
**NEST TYPE:** GLOWING GRASS
**FLIGHT ABILITY:** 3

**SAVANNAH**

# ZEBRUSH
## (PURPLE)

**FUN FACT:**
Purple Zebrush likes to change up her look with EGGSquisite new styles!

**DID YOU KNOW?**
Purple Zebrush changes her mane to suit her moods!

**SEASON:** 1
**RARITY:** Common
**NEST TYPE:** GLOWING GRASS
**FLIGHT ABILITY:** 3

SAVANNAH

# CHEETREE
## (ORANGE)

**FUN FACT:**
Orange Cheetree loves to be active. She's always playing new sports, and she organizes a weekly game of Hatchy Ball.

**SEASON:** 2
**RARITY:** common
**NEST TYPE:** GLOWING GRASS
**FLIGHT ABILITY:** 5

**DID YOU KNOW?**
Orange Cheetree is the top scorer on the Savannah Hatchy Ball team!

# CHEETREE
## (YELLOW)

**FUN FACT:**
Yellow Cheetree is super speedy. He travels to as many spots around Hatchtopia as he can in one day.

**DID YOU KNOW?**
Yellow Cheetree helps deliver letters all over Hatchtopia!

**SEASON:** 2
**RARITY:** RARE
**NEST TYPE:** GLOWING GRASS
**FLIGHT ABILITY:** 4

# DRAGGLE
## (PINK)

**FUN FACT:**
Pink Draggle knows the most about the magic of Hatchtopia!

**DID YOU KNOW?**
She helps new Hatchimals make wishes at Wishing Star Waterfall!

**SEASON:** 2
**RARITY:** common
**NEST TYPE:** SPARKLING SAND
**FLIGHT ABILITY:** 5

# SAVANNAH

# ELEFLY
## (PINK)

**FUN FACT:**
On the hottest days, Pink Elefly searches out new watering holes. Then she uses her trunk as a sprinkler to keep her friends cool.

**SEASON:** 2
**RARITY:** common
**NEST TYPE:** SPARKLING SAND
**FLIGHT ABILITY:** 3

**DID YOU KNOW?**
Pink Elefly loves to vacation at Breezy Beach!

83

SAVANNAH

# GIRREO
## (PURPLE)

**FUN FACT:**

Purple Girreo gets her heart pumping by attending dance classes at Fabula Forest.

**SEASON:** 2
**RARITY:** common
**NEST TYPE:** GLOWING GRASS
**FLIGHT ABILITY:** 3

**DID YOU KNOW?**

Purple Girreo drinks a healthy wheatgrass smoothie for breakfast every day!

# RHOOBY
## (BLUE)

**FUN FACT:**

Blue Rhooby loves to take care of the Cushy Cacti and make sure they have what they need to grow!

**DID YOU KNOW?**

Blue Rhooby likes to tiptoe through the sparkly sand.

**SEASON:** 2
**RARITY:** common
**NEST TYPE:** SPARKLING SAND
**FLIGHT ABILITY:** 1

## RHOOBY
### (PURPLE)

### FUN FACT:
Purple Rhooby is curious about the world and loves to share the things she learns. That's why she's a teacher at the Daisy Schoolhouse.

**DID YOU KNOW?**
Purple Rhooby's favorite subject is Hatchy History!

**SEASON:** 2
**RARITY:** ULTRA RARE
**NEST TYPE:** SPARKLING SAND
**FLIGHT ABILITY:** 2

**SAVANNAH**

## ZEBRUSH
### (GREEN)

### FUN FACT:
Green Zebrush is always ready to try something new—like hunting for hidden treasures in Crystal Canyon.

**DID YOU KNOW?**
Green Zebrush makes bracelets out of Crystal Canyon gems!

**SEASON:** 2
**RARITY:** RARE
**NEST TYPE:** GLOWING GRASS
**FLIGHT ABILITY:** 3

# SIZZLING SPOTS

SAVANNAH

# DESERT

There's nothing like a Hatchtastic day spent in the desert! This sunny spot is one of the hottest locations in all of Hatchtopia, and the Desert family likes it that way! They love the feeling of the sand beneath their feet and the hot sun on their glittery wings. The Hatchimals who live here are as warm as the place they call home!

These smart, tough creatures always do what it takes to get things done. But as much as they want to get out of any tricky spot they may find themselves in, the Desert Hatchimals would never step on anyone's toes. They get along with **a smile of friendship and a helping paw.**

DESERT

# KOALABEE
## (BLUE)

**FUN FACT:**
Blue Koalabee is a scientific leader who blazes a path to new discoveries.

**SEASON:** 1
**RARITY:** COMMON
**NEST TYPE:** WARMING WILLOW
**FLIGHT ABILITY:** 3

**DID YOU KNOW?**
Blue Koalabee works hard to explain all the things that magic can't.

# KOALABEE
## (PURPLE)

**FUN FACT:**
Purple Koalabee's down-to-earth attitude and at-the-ready toolbox mean he always gets the job done.

**DID YOU KNOW?**
Purple Koalabee partners with Yellow Crabler to hatch plans for new designs!

**SEASON:** 1
**RARITY:** COMMON
**NEST TYPE:** WARMING WILLOW
**FLIGHT ABILITY:** 3

## ARMADILLARK
### (GREEN)

**FUN FACT:**
Green Armadillark loves sliding down the sand dunes on her shell!

**DID YOU KNOW?**
Green Armadillark is also a great tobEGGaner!

**SEASON:** 2
**RARITY:** COMMON
**NEST TYPE:** CUSHY CACTUS
**FLIGHT ABILITY:** 2

## ARMADILLARK
### (YELLOW)

**FUN FACT:**
Yellow Armadillark likes to chill. She's always working on her tan in the hot desert sun.

**DID YOU KNOW?**
Yellow Armadillark could spend every day at Breezy Beach!

**SEASON:** 2
**RARITY:** ULTRA RARE
**NEST TYPE:** CUSHY CACTUS
**FLIGHT ABILITY:** 2

# CAMELARK
## (MAGENTA)

**FUN FACT:**
Magenta Camelark loves to stargaze. His favorite hobby is watching shooting stars get caught in Wishing Star Waterfall.

**SEASON:** 2
**RARITY:** RARE
**NEST TYPE:** TUMBLEWEED
**FLIGHT ABILITY:** 3

**DID YOU KNOW?**
Magenta Camelark would love to discover life on another planet!

# CAMELARK
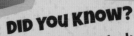
## (YELLOW)

**FUN FACT:**
Yellow Camelark loves to eat. Her favorite thing is a big feast with all her favorite foods . . . and her friends!

**DID YOU KNOW?**
Yellow Camelark runs the Hatchtopia Foodies' Club!

**SEASON:** 2
**RARITY:** COMMON
**NEST TYPE:** TUMBLEWEED
**FLIGHT ABILITY:** 2

# KANGAROOSE
## (BLUE)

### FUN FACT:
Blue Kangaroose always speaks her mind. She's very trustworthy and tells it like it is!

### DID YOU KNOW?
Blue Kangaroose is a judge at the Hatchy Games!

**SEASON:** 2
**RARITY:** common
**NEST TYPE:** TUMBLEWEED
**FLIGHT ABILITY:** 3

**DESERT**

# KANGAROOSE
## (PURPLE)

### FUN FACT:
Purple Kangaroose has endless energy. She's a hopscotch champion who loves the Breathless Bouncing Ball Festival!

### DID YOU KNOW?
Purple Kangaroose loves to fly up and bounce on the clouds!

**SEASON:** 2
**RARITY:** common
**NEST TYPE:** TUMBLEWEED
**FLIGHT ABILITY:** 3

# SANDSNAKE
## (BLUE)

**FUN FACT:**

Blue Sandsnake may sometimes get himself into a little bit of trouble, but he also has a warm and loving heart.

**SEASON:** 2
**RARITY:** RARE
**NEST TYPE:** WARMING WILLOW
**FLIGHT ABILITY:** 4

**DID YOU KNOW?**

Blue Sandsnake often sssneaks out for a midnight snack!

# SANDSNAKE
## (GREEN)

**FUN FACT:**

Green Sandsnake has a super sense of smell!

**DID YOU KNOW?**

Green Sandsnake always knows when treats are nearby.

**SEASON:** 2
**RARITY:** COMMON
**NEST TYPE:** WARMING WILLOW
**FLIGHT ABILITY:** 5

# DESERT DUOS

# RIVER

Surrounded by Lily Logs, Silk Shrubs, and Seaweed, River Hatchimals like to lounge around and laugh with friends while floating through the calm water. Playful and funny, the Hatchimals of the River family are silly creatures who **love a good joke.** Above all, Hatchimals who hang out here feel best near the water, where they can relax on the riverbank or raft downstream!

These are some of their favorite jokes:

HOW DO YOU MAKE AN OCTAPITTA LAUGH?

WITH TEN-TICKLES!

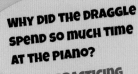

WHY DID THE DRAGGLE SPEND SO MUCH TIME AT THE PIANO?

IT WAS PRACTICING ITS SCALES!

WHERE DO POLAR PENGUALAS KEEP THEIR MONEY?

IN THE SNOW BANK!

River Hatchimals are also incredibly kindhearted. **They would do anything to make their friends smile.** No matter what new situation these Hatchimals find themselves in, their humor and happy-go-lucky attitude mean they always **make a splash.**

# FLAMINGOOSE
## (MAGENTA)

### FUN FACT:
Magenta Flamingoose is loyal to her friends. She'll always stand up for them, sometimes on one leg!

**SEASON:** 1*
**RARITY:** Common
**NEST TYPE:** LILY LOG
**FLIGHT ABILITY:** 4

**DID YOU KNOW?**
Magenta Flamingoose loves to float lazily down the river.

RIVER

# FLAMINGOOSE
## (PURPLE)

### FUN FACT:
Purple Flamingoose is tranquil and serene. She leads yoga classes by the water for all her friends.

**SEASON:** 1*
**RARITY:** Common
**NEST TYPE:** LILY LOG
**FLIGHT ABILITY:** 4

**DID YOU KNOW?**
Purple Flamingoose meditates every morning!

95

*Exclusive to Season 1 12-pack egg carton

# HIPHATCH (BLUE)

**FUN FACT:**
Blue Hiphatch plays silly practical jokes on her friends.

**SEASON:** 1
**RARITY:** common
**NEST TYPE:** SILK SHRUB
**FLIGHT ABILITY:** 1

**DID YOU KNOW?**
Blue Hiphatch never pranks the same Hatchimal twice!

# HIPHATCH (PINK)

**FUN FACT:**
Pink Hiphatch knows what she wants and goes after it!

**DID YOU KNOW?**
Pink Hiphatch likes to do cannonballs into the river!

**SEASON:** 1
**RARITY:** ULTRA RARE
**NEST TYPE:** SILK SHRUB
**FLIGHT ABILITY:** 3

# SWOTTER
## (PURPLE)

**FUN FACT:**
Purple Swotter likes to float hand in hand with his HFF.

**DID YOU KNOW?**
His HFF is Red Swotter!

**SEASON:** 1
**RARITY:** RARE
**NEST TYPE:** LILY LOG
**FLIGHT ABILITY:** 5

# SWOTTER
## (RED)

**FUN FACT:**
Red Swotter is EGGStremely curious. There isn't a riddle she can't crack!

**DID YOU KNOW?**
Red Swotter loves to read mysteries!

**SEASON:** 1
**RARITY:** Common
**NEST TYPE:** LILY LOG
**FLIGHT ABILITY:** 1

# Beaveery
## (ORANGE)

**FUN FACT:**

Orange Beaveery is very supportive of her friends. She's always ready to lend a helping paw.

**SEASON:** 2
**RARITY:** common
**NEST TYPE:** LILY LOG
**FLIGHT ABILITY:** 2

**RIVER**

**DID YOU KNOW?**

Orange Beaveery sends heartfelt letters to her closest pals every week!

# Beaveery
## (TEAL)

**FUN FACT:**

Teal Beaveery can carve a log into a canoe, basket, or work of art with nothing more than a little chomp of her teeth.

**DID YOU KNOW?**

Teal Beaveery always carries a toothbrush— just in case!

**SEASON:** 2
**RARITY:** RARE
**NEST TYPE:** LILY LOG
**FLIGHT ABILITY:** 3

98

## DUCKLE (BLUE)

### FUN FACT:
Blue Duckle writes amazing poems for her one true love. But she'll never tell which Hatchimal that is . . .

**DID YOU KNOW?**
Blue Duckle loves romantic movies!

**SEASON: 2**
**RARITY: COMMON**
**NEST TYPE: SILK SHRUB**
**FLIGHT ABILITY: 4**

## DUCKLE (GREEN)

### FUN FACT:
Green Duckle lets everything roll off his back. Spending a tranquil day at Cloud Cove is his favorite way to relax and take it easy.

**SEASON: 2**
**RARITY: COMMON**
**NEST TYPE: SILK SHRUB**
**FLIGHT ABILITY: 4**

**DID YOU KNOW?**
Green Duckle's nickname is Quackers!

RIVER

# FIGEON (BLUE)

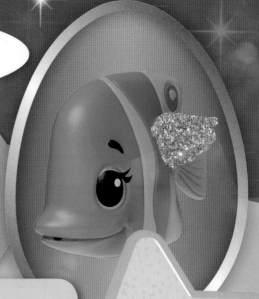

**FUN FACT:**
Blue Figeon has a hard time being serious. He can't help trying to get a laugh.

**SEASON:** 2
**RARITY:** RARE
**NEST TYPE:** SEAWEED
**FLIGHT ABILITY:** 2

**DID YOU KNOW?**
Blue Figeon is the ultimate prankster of Hatchtopia!

# FIGEON (ORANGE)

**FUN FACT:**
Orange Figeon always encourages friends to come out of their shell!

**DID YOU KNOW?**
Orange Figeon's confidence comes from within!

**SEASON:** 2
**RARITY:** RARE
**NEST TYPE:** SEAWEED
**FLIGHT ABILITY:** 1

100

# FLAMINGOOSE
## (FUCHSIA)

**FUN FACT:**
Fuchsia Flamingoose always has her head in the clouds!

**DID YOU KNOW?**
Fuchsia Flamingoose loves to fly over Hatchtopia to see what's going on around the world!

**SEASON:** 2
**RARITY:** Common
**NEST TYPE:** LILY LOG
**FLIGHT ABILITY:** 4

RIVER

# FLAMINGOOSE
## (PINK)

**FUN FACT:**
Pink Flamingoose loves bright colors, feathery costumes, and showing off her skills on the dance floor.

**DID YOU KNOW?**
Pink Flamingoose enjoys the spotlight!

**SEASON:** 2
**RARITY:** Common
**NEST TYPE:** LILY LOG
**FLIGHT ABILITY:** 3

# HIPHATCH
## (PURPLE)

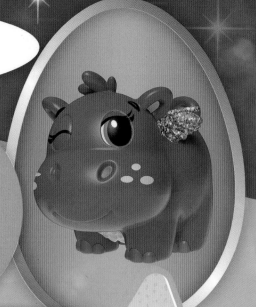

**FUN FACT:**
The only thing Purple Hiphatch likes more than telling a joke is hearing one. His booming laugh can be heard from Shimmering Sands all the way to Cloud Cove.

**RIVER**

**SEASON:** 2
**RARITY:** Common
**NEST TYPE:** SILK SHRUB
**FLIGHT ABILITY:** 2

**DID YOU KNOW?**
Purple Hiphatch loves singing karaoke!

# PLATYPIPER
## (GREEN)

**FUN FACT:**
Green Platypiper lives for rock and roll. She's got rhythm from the tip of her bill to the webs of her feet!

**DID YOU KNOW?**
Green Platypiper writes her own songs and plays the guitar!

**SEASON:** 2
**RARITY:** ULTRA RARE
**NEST TYPE:** LILY LOG
**FLIGHT ABILITY:** 3

# PLATYPIPER
## (PINK)

**FUN FACT:**
Pink Platypiper loves rafting down the river!

**DID YOU KNOW?**
Teal Beaveery gave Pink Platypiper her first canoe!

**SEASON:** 2
**RARITY:** common
**NEST TYPE:** LILY LOG
**FLIGHT ABILITY:** 3

# SWOTTER
## (BLUE)

**FUN FACT:**
Blue Swotter glides through the water with grace and style.

**DID YOU KNOW?**
Blue Swotter has a swimming cap in every color of the rainbow!

**SEASON:** 2
**RARITY:** common
**NEST TYPE:** LILY LOG
**FLIGHT ABILITY:** 3

# SWIMMING SWEETIES

# POLAR PARADISE

When the Hatchimals want to chill, they head to Polar Paradise—**the coolest place in Hatchtopia!** With its ice-covered mountaintops and gently falling snowflakes, it's the perfect place to ski down **Glacial Peak,** start a snowball fight with friends, or cozy up with a steaming mug of cocoa.

## The Special Edition translucent Hatchimals

of Polar Paradise love nothing more than playing in the fresh white powder that blankets the ground. Whether they're making snow angels, crafting ice sculptures, or tobEGGaning through the frosty hills, Polar Hatchimals know they'll always have fun in the snow!

POLAR PARADISE

# POLAR DRAGGLE

**FUN FACT:**
It's hard to ruffle Polar Draggle's scales. She's as cool as a Crystal Cucumber!

**SEASON:** 1
**RARITY:** RARE
**NEST TYPE:** FOREVERGREEN TREE
**FLIGHT ABILITY:** 4

**DID YOU KNOW?**
Polar Draggle's favorite treat is a tasty snow cone!

# POLAR FOXFIN

**FUN FACT:**
Polar Foxfin likes to EGGSplore new heights in Polar Paradise!

**DID YOU KNOW?**
Polar Foxfin is an EGGSpert snowboarder!

**SEASON:** 1
**RARITY:** RARE
**NEST TYPE:** COCONUT SNOW
**FLIGHT ABILITY:** 4

# POLAR HUMMINGBEAR

**FUN FACT:**
Polar Hummingbear loves to do arts and crafts. The messier, the better!

**DID YOU KNOW?**
Polar Hummingbear is famous for her papier-mâché snowflakes!

**SEASON:** 1
**RARITY:** ULTRA RARE
**NEST TYPE:** FOREVERGREEN TREE
**FLIGHT ABILITY:** 2

# POLAR PENGUALA

**FUN FACT:**
Polar Penguala is a thrill seeker with a competitive streak—she's the reigning ski-jump champion!

**DID YOU KNOW?**
Polar Penguala likes to make snow angels!

**SEASON:** 1
**RARITY:** RARE
**NEST TYPE:** FOREVERGREEN TREE
**FLIGHT ABILITY:** 4

POLAR PARADISE

107

POLAR PARADISE

# POLAR SEALARK

**FUN FACT:**
When Polar Sealark is around, the big laughs never end. She's always quick to crack an EGGcellent joke for her friends.

**SEASON:** 1
**RARITY:** RARE
**NEST TYPE:** COCONUT SNOW
**FLIGHT ABILITY:** 2

**DID YOU KNOW?**
Polar Sealark likes to slide on the ice and jump into snow banks!

# POLAR SWHALE

**FUN FACT:**
It's important to Polar Swhale to be kind to everyone he meets!

**DID YOU KNOW?**
Polar Swhale loves to visit Snowflake Shire!

**SEASON:** 1
**RARITY:** RARE
**NEST TYPE:** ENCHANTED ICE
**FLIGHT ABILITY:** 1

# WINTER WONDERLAND

# LILAC LAKE

Shimmering in glorious shades of lavender, amethyst, and magenta, Lilac Lake offers Hatchimals **a place to unwind** and have a great time splashing around and enjoying the water sports that life on the lake has to offer. And when Hatchimals jump off **Lilac Dock** to take a dip in the lake's cool waters, they turn a glistening purple . . . at least for a while! That's why the Hatchimals that hang out here are always purple!

Because of Lilac Lake's magic color-changing properties, Hatchimals love to plan amazing art projects on its shores. If they want to paint a beautiful picture of the lake, they only have to dip their brushes in the water to capture its **special purple hue.**

# LILAC BUNWEE

**FUN FACT:**
Lilac Bunwee is a shining star who always lights up a room with her bright smile and charming stories.

**DID YOU KNOW?**
Lilac Bunwee makes lilac lemonade from the lake's purple water!

**SEASON:** 1
**RARITY:** common
**NEST TYPE:** PINK FLORA
**FLIGHT ABILITY:** 3

# LILAC GIRREO

**FUN FACT:**
Lilac Girreo is the tallest of all her friends!

**SEASON:** 1
**RARITY:** common
**NEST TYPE:** VIOLET VINES
**FLIGHT ABILITY:** 3

**DID YOU KNOW?**
Lilac Girreo loves diving off Lilac Dock!

111

LILAC LAKE

# LILAC HEDGYHen

**FUN FACT:**
Lilac Hedgyhen is soft both inside and out!

**season:** 1
**RARITY:** ULTRA RARE
**NEST TYPE:** PINK FLORA
**FLIGHT ABILITY:** 3

**DID YOU KNOW?**
Lilac Hedgyhen would do anything to protect her friends!

# LILAC PENGUALA

**FUN FACT:**
Lilac Penguala always seems to know what her friends are thinking.

**DID YOU KNOW?**
Lilac Penguala loves surprises!

**season:** 1
**RARITY:** RARE
**NEST TYPE:** VIOLET VINES
**FLIGHT ABILITY:** 4

## LILAC SWHALE

**FUN FACT:**
Lilac Swhale is the best at singing underwater!

**DID YOU KNOW?**
Lilac Swhale is learning to fly with the help of Lilac Penguala!

**SEASON:** 1
**RARITY:** RARE
**NEST TYPE:** VIOLET VINES
**FLIGHT ABILITY:** 2

## LILAC TIGRETTE

**FUN FACT:**
Lilac Tigrette swims in Lilac Lake to relax after a big adventure.

**DID YOU KNOW?**
Lilac Tigrette leads an adventure club!

**SEASON:** 1
**RARITY:** COMMON
**NEST TYPE:** VIOLET VINES
**FLIGHT ABILITY:** 2

PURPLE PASSION

LILAC LAKE

# GIGGLE GROVE

**The heart of Hatchtopia** can be found at Giggle Grove. It's an enchanted place that lifts the spirits of the Hatchimals who visit. That's because it's home to the famous **Giggling Tree**, whose magic spreads laughter and cheer across Hatchtopia. It also has a **magical door** in its trunk that connects Hatchtopia to our world!

With a tickling wind, the Giggling Tree erupts into a fit of melodious laughter. Every giggle from the tree releases a magical, teardrop-shaped seed. These seeds are important—they grow into new trees that give Hatchimal eggs a place to nest.

When the Hatchimals need a good chuckle, they visit their friends at **Giggle Grove**, who are always a bundle of fun! Their positive attitude makes them an absolute pleasure to be around. Hatchimals who hang out here are bursting with happiness, and they love to share that flying-high feeling!

GIGGLE GROVE

# GIGGLING DRAGGLE

**FUN FACT:**
Giggling Draggle is a creative thinker and creator—when he's not distracted, anyway!

**SEASON:** 1
**RARITY:** Common
**NEST TYPE:** GIGGLING TREE
**FLIGHT ABILITY:** 5

**DID YOU KNOW?**
Giggling Draggle is the youngest member of Team Hatch.

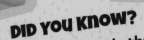

# GIGGLING ELEFLY

**FUN FACT:**
Giggling Elefly never forgets a good joke!

**DID YOU KNOW?**
Giggling Elefly's ears bounce up and down as she laughs!

**SEASON:** 1
**RARITY:** RARE
**NEST TYPE:** GIGGLING TREE
**FLIGHT ABILITY:** 4

# GIGGLING PANDOR

## FUN FACT:
Giggling Pandor is beloved across Hatchtopia because she's sweet and totally huggable!

**SEASON:** 1
**RARITY:** common
**NEST TYPE:** GIGGLING TREE
**FLIGHT ABILITY:** 3

**DID YOU KNOW?**
Giggling Pandor gives out the sweetest compliments!

GIGGLE GROVE

# GIGGLING PENGUALA

## FUN FACT:
Giggling Penguala says what's on her mind, but she's always super positive!

**SEASON:** 1
**RARITY:** common
**NEST TYPE:** GIGGLING TREE
**FLIGHT ABILITY:** 3

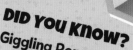

**DID YOU KNOW?**
Giggling Penguala is constantly cracking jokes!

GIGGLE GROVE

# GIGGLING RASPOON

**FUN FACT:**
Giggling Raspoon has a huge heart. He loves to welcome visitors to Hatchtopia.

**SEASON: 1**
**RARITY: ULTRA RARE**
**NEST TYPE: GIGGLING TREE**
**FLIGHT ABILITY: 3**

**DID YOU KNOW?**
Giggling Raspoon makes up a secret handshake with every newcomer!

# GIGGLING ZEBRUSH

**FUN FACT:**
Giggling Zebrush thinks the best of everyone!

**DID YOU KNOW?**
Giggling Zebrush believes honesty is the best policy!

**SEASON: 1**
**RARITY: common**
**NEST TYPE: GIGGLING TREE**
**FLIGHT ABILITY: 3**

# HAPPY HATCHIMALS

# CLOUD COVE

**High up in the sky,** there lies a magical island made of cottony clouds that are softer than a Bunwee's tail and lighter than a Chickchaff's feather. Cloud Cove is the perfect spot for Hatchimals to rest when their glittery wings tire of flying. Whether they stop by for a quick nap or a longer hibernation, Hatchimals are always happy to kick back in Cloud Cove.

All Hatchimals can fly. But the Hatchimals who hang out here soar higher than the rest! They are the best flyers in Hatchtopia, and rolling around in the clouds gives them their soft coats. Their wings are strong and their hearts even stronger. They watch over all their friends from up above!

# CLOUD DRAGGLE

**FUN FACT:**
Cloud Draggle is a sky sculptor and makes beautiful shapes out of the clouds.

**DID YOU KNOW?**
Cloud Draggle draws inspiration for his sculptures from his HFFs!

**SEASON:** 1
**RARITY:** LIMITED
**NEST TYPE:** CASHMERE CLOUDS
**FLIGHT ABILITY:** 5

# CLOUD KITTYCAN

**FUN FACT:**
Cloud Kittycan has tons of energy. She is always pouncing and bouncing around!

**DID YOU KNOW?**
Cloud Kittycan prefers playtime to naptime!

**SEASON:** 1
**RARITY:** LIMITED
**NEST TYPE:** CASHMERE CLOUDS
**FLIGHT ABILITY:** 5

121

CLOUD COVE

# CLOUD LEORIOLE

**FUN FACT:**
Cloud Leoriole may look furr-ocious, but he's one of the biggest softies in Hatchtopia!

**SEASON:** 1
**RARITY:** LIMITED
**NEST TYPE:** CASHMERE CLOUDS
**FLIGHT ABILITY:** 5

**DID YOU KNOW?**
Cloud Leoriole has the cutest little roar.

## CLOUD PIGPIPER

**FUN FACT:**
Cloud Pigpiper is the most ticklish of all the Hatchimals!

**DID YOU KNOW?**
Cloud Pigpiper gives piggybacks to those who have trouble flying high!

**SEASON:** 1
**RARITY:** LIMITED
**NEST TYPE:** CASHMERE CLOUDS
**FLIGHT ABILITY:** 5

# CLOUD PONETTE

**FUN FACT:**
Cloud Ponette loves to race in the clouds with his best friends!

**DID YOU KNOW?**
Cloud Ponette is an EGGSpert at doing loop-the-loops!

**SEASON: 1**
**RARITY: LIMITED**
**NEST TYPE: CASHMERE CLOUDS**
**FLIGHT ABILITY: 5**

CLOUD COVE

# CLOUD PUPPIT

**FUN FACT:**
Cloud Puppit is a loyal friend who will fly anywhere for those she loves.

**SEASON: 1**
**RARITY: LIMITED**
**NEST TYPE: CASHMERE CLOUDS**
**FLIGHT ABILITY: 5**

**DID YOU KNOW?**
The water from Cloud Cove trickles down into Wishing Star Waterfall!

123

# FLYING FLUFFY FRIENDS

# SNOWFLAKE SHIRE

Hatchimals flock to Snowflake Shire when they need a little **cozy comfort.** This charming cottage can be found **nestled in the mountains of Polar Paradise.** It's a warm, welcoming refuge where Hatchimals can gather round a roaring fire, drink mugs of hot cocoa with snowflake-shaped marshmallows, and tell stories of their adventures.

In fact, Snowflake Shire is home to Hatchtopia's **annual storytelling contest.** Hatchimals from all over the world come to tell their funniest fables and spookiest ghost stories to a packed house!

Snowflake Shire has a secret. The snowflakes that swirl around the shire are as slippery as ice and blow faster than the winter wind. But if a Hatchimal can catch one before it touches the snow-covered ground, **the snowflake will pass along its glistening magic.** That's why the Hatchimals who hang out at the shire glimmer like pearls. They are sweet and bubbly and never pass up an opportunity to let their inner light shine!

# SNOWFLAKE BELUGULL

**FUN FACT:**
Snowflake Belugull cares about her environment. She makes sure the water in every lake, pool, and ocean stays clean and healthy.

**SEASON:** 2
**RARITY:** ULTRA RARE
**NEST TYPE:** ENCHANTED ICE
**FLIGHT ABILITY:** 2

**DID YOU KNOW?**
Snowflake Belugull is one of the best cold-water swimmers in Snowflake Shire!

# SNOWFLAKE HUMMINGBEAR

**FUN FACT:**
Snowflake Hummingbear has won the annual storytelling contest two years in a row!

**DID YOU KNOW?**
Snowflake Hummingbear's favorite fairy tale is called *Belugull and the Beast.*

**SEASON:** 2
**RARITY:** RARE
**NEST TYPE:** FOREVERGREEN TREE
**FLIGHT ABILITY:** 2

# Snowflake NARWARBLER

## FUN FACT:
Snowflake Narwarbler may be the strongest Hatchimal on Glacial Peak, but she's also the nicest!

## DID YOU KNOW?
She once rescued Snowflake Penguala from drifting on an iceberg!

**SEASON:** 2
**RARITY:** RARE
**NEST TYPE:** ENCHANTED ICE
**FLIGHT ABILITY:** 4

# Snowflake PENGUALA

## FUN FACT:
Snowflake Penguala loves to dance—even when there's no music!

## DID YOU KNOW?
Snowflake Penguala always has a waddle in her step!

**SEASON:** 2
**RARITY:** RARE
**NEST TYPE:** FOREVERGREEN TREE
**FLIGHT ABILITY:** 5

127

SNOWFLAKE SHIRE

# SNOWFLAKE SEALARK

**FUN FACT:**
Snowflake Sealark is fierce and fearless. No feat is too scary for her!

**SEASON:** 2
**RARITY:** RARE
**NEST TYPE:** COCONUT SNOW
**FLIGHT ABILITY:** 3

**DID YOU KNOW?**
Snowflake Sealark leads flying tours around Snowflake Shire!

# SNOWFLAKE WALWREN

**FUN FACT:**
Snowflake Walwren is one of the chattiest Hatchimals in the shire!

**DID YOU KNOW?**
She's one of the judges in the annual storytelling contest!

**SEASON:** 2
**RARITY:** RARE
**NEST TYPE:** COCONUT SNOW
**FLIGHT ABILITY:** 2

# WINTER BREAK

# MAGICAL MEADOW

Luscious pastures of **Lullaby Grass** and downy-soft dandelions make Magical Meadow an ideal location to **frolic through the fields or daydream the days away.** It's a quiet, pretty spot where Hatchimals can feel comfy and content. It's also the perfect place for sharing secrets. Hatchimals just have to whisper the words, and a gentle breeze will carry their message to a friend.

Hatchimals love coming to Magical Meadow to lie back in the grass and watch the clouds above them. Sometimes, when the meadow is at its most magical, **the clouds put on a show,** with cottony critters having fun adventures in the sky.

The Hatchimals who hang out at Magical Meadow have nice, fuzzy coats, and these **soft sweeties** are always gentle and kind. They can't help but spread happiness wherever they go!

# MAGICAL BUDGIBY (YELLOW)

## FUN FACT:
This Magical Budgiby spots everything. She notices if even one grain at Shimmering Sands has been moved!

### DID YOU KNOW?
She treasures her jeweled magnifying glass!

**SEASON:** 2
**RARITY:** LIMITED
**NEST TYPE:** EUCALYPTUS TREE
**FLIGHT ABILITY:** 5

# MAGICAL BUDGIBY (GREEN)

## FUN FACT:
Magical Budgiby loves a surprise, especially planning secret birthday parties for his friends!

**SEASON:** 2
**RARITY:** LIMITED
**NEST TYPE:** EUCALYPTUS TREE
**FLIGHT ABILITY:** 5

### DID YOU KNOW?
Magical Budgiby loves taking photos of friends to capture their reactions to his surprises!

# MAGICAL MEADOW

## MAGICAL FARROW (PINK)

**FUN FACT:**
Magical Farrow is cheerful and kind. Her smile sweetens everyone's day!

**Season:** 2
**RARITY:** Secret
**NEST TYPE:** EUCALYPTUS TREE
**FLIGHT ABILITY:** 4

**DID YOU KNOW?**
She runs the local bakery and loves trying out new recipes!

## MAGICAL FARROW (GREEN)

**FUN FACT:**
Magical Farrow knows her way around a toolbox. She can fix almost anything in a jiffy!

**DID YOU KNOW?**
She's been all over Hatchtopia to help friends and is known as Miss Fix-It!

**Season:** 2
**RARITY:** Secret
**NEST TYPE:** EUCALYPTUS TREE
**FLIGHT ABILITY:** 4

# MAGICAL HAMSTAR
## (BLUE)

**FUN FACT:**
Magical Hamstar loves taking care of all the flowers in the meadow!

**DID YOU KNOW?**
She hosts slumber parties in the Lullaby Grass for all her friends!

**SEASON:** 2
**RARITY:** LIMITED
**NEST TYPE:** LULLABY GRASS
**FLIGHT ABILITY:** 3

# MAGICAL HAMSTAR
## (PINK)

**FUN FACT:**
Magical Hamstar likes to create art in the most unusual spots. You can find her paintings hidden among the rocks at Magical Meadow!

**SEASON:** 2
**RARITY:** LIMITED
**NEST TYPE:** LULLABY GRASS
**FLIGHT ABILITY:** 2

**DID YOU KNOW?**
She makes all of her paint out of the flowers!

MAGICAL MEADOW

133

MAGICAL MEADOW

# MAGICAL KITTYCAN

**FUN FACT:**
Magical Kittycan is active in the EGGStreme. When she's not climbing the trees of Fabula Forest, she's pouncing on her friends to play!

**SEASON:** 2
**RARITY:** LIMITED
**NEST TYPE:** LULLABY GRASS
**FLIGHT ABILITY:** 3

**DID YOU KNOW?**
Her next goal is to climb Glacial Peak!

# MAGICAL PUPPIT

**FUN FACT:**
Magical Puppit is a natural leader with a brave streak and a nose for trouble.

**DID YOU KNOW?**
Magical Puppit is one of Hatchtopia's firefighters!

**SEASON:** 2
**RARITY:** LIMITED
**NEST TYPE:** LULLABY GRASS
**FLIGHT ABILITY:** 3

# PLAYFUL PLANTS

# GLITTERING GARDEN

When the Hatchimals want to stop and smell the roses, they come to **Glittering Garden,** where the lush flower patch sparkles in the sunshine. With Eightlips that give kisses and Buttercups dripping with real butter, you never know what kinds of magic will sprout here!

That's why Glittering Garden is the perfect place to host the Hatchimals' annual **Springtime Tea Party.** Hatchimals sip tasty tea while sitting among Silly Lilies, hoping to spot the rare Oopsy-Daisy that never grows in the same place twice. Glittering Garden is also home to the **Daisy Schoolhouse,** where learning is truly magical. The school's Blue-Bell calls students to class so their studies can begin!

The Hatchimals who hang out here all have glittery bodies and a flair for the dramatic! They love facing big challenges and trying new things! And these Hatchimals know how to **add some sparkle to any occasion.** It's never a dull moment with friends like these around!

# GLITTERING ALBASLOTH

## FUN FACT:

Glittering Albasloth loves flying high in the sky and seeing the beautiful garden from above.

### DID YOU KNOW?
Glittering Albasloth loves to wear sparkly outfits!

**SEASON:** 1
**RARITY:** Common
**NEST TYPE:** Dazzle Dune
**FLIGHT ABILITY:** 5

# GLITTERING CRABLER

## FUN FACT:
Glittering Crabler loves swimming almost as much as she loves to garden! That's why she's always visiting Breezy Beach!

**SEASON:** 1
**RARITY:** Common
**NEST TYPE:** Dazzle Dune
**FLIGHT ABILITY:** 4

### DID YOU KNOW?
She's been teaching Blue Seaspoon about gardening!

# GLITTERING DUCKLE

GLITTERING GARDEN

**FUN FACT:**
Happy-go-lucky Glittering Duckle has a positive attitude. She's always cheerful and carefree!

**SEASON:** 1
**RARITY:** Common
**NEST TYPE:** Dazzle Dune
**FLIGHT ABILITY:** 4

**DID YOU KNOW?**
Glittering Duckle's favorite color is glitter!

# GLITTERING PLATYPIPER

**FUN FACT:**
Glittering Platypiper makes beautiful flower crowns for all her friends!

**DID YOU KNOW?**
She wished for a new flower at Wishing Star Waterfall. That's how Silly Lilies started growing!

**SEASON:** 1
**RARITY:** Common
**NEST TYPE:** Dazzle Dune
**FLIGHT ABILITY:** 3

# GLITTERING RHOOBY

## FUN FACT:
Glittering Rhooby makes the best tea at the Springtime Tea Party, using rare flowers from the garden!

## DID YOU KNOW?
She's the best at finding the Oopsy-Daisy flower!

**SEASON:** 1
**RARITY:** Common
**NEST TYPE:** ROCK GARDEN
**FLIGHT ABILITY:** 2

# GLITTERING WALWREN

## FUN FACT:
Glittering Walwren is always making sure Glittering Garden is as beautiful as can be!

## DID YOU KNOW?
Glittering Walwren's secret is to water the flowers with Lilac Lake's glistening purple water!

**SEASON:** 1
**RARITY:** Common
**NEST TYPE:** ROCK GARDEN
**FLIGHT ABILITY:** 2

139

# GLITTERING
# GETAWAYS

# CRYSTAL CANYON

Nestled in the mountains, Crystal Canyon shines good fortune over Hatchtopia. **Rare jewels** of all shapes and sizes can be found tucked inside its crevasses. The canyon is made of enchanted translucent crystals that reflect **luck and happiness** on anyone who views them. But most magical of all are the mood crystal nests that change how Hatchimals feel when they sit in them. Yellow represents happiness, green is serenity, purple is courage, blue is strength, red is wisdom, and pink is love.

The Hatchimals who hang out here have sparkling personalities and jeweled bodies. Their pearls of wisdom help their friends truly shine.

# CRYSTAL BEAVEERY

**FUN FACT:**
Crystal Beaveery makes beautiful jewelry out of the gems in the canyon.

**SEASON:** 2
**RARITY:** common
**NEST TYPE:** CRYSTALLine
**FLIGHT ABILITY:** 2

**DID YOU KNOW?**
She once made a tiara for Crystal Octapitta's Hatchy Birthday party!

# CRYSTAL BUTTERPUFF

**FUN FACT:**
Crystal Butterpuff loves to feel the breeze flutter through her wings on long leisurely flights.

**DID YOU KNOW?**
Crystal Butterpuff sits in the yellow crystal nest for EGGStra happiness!

**SEASON:** 2
**RARITY:** common
**NEST TYPE:** CRYSTALLine
**FLIGHT ABILITY:** 5

# CRYSTAL CHAMELOON

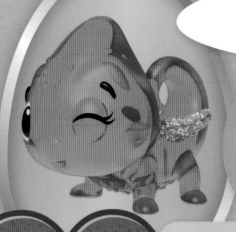

**FUN FACT:**
Crystal Chameloon is trying to be less shy and more confident!

**DID YOU KNOW?**
She sits in the purple crystal nests to become more courageous!

**SEASON:** 2
**RARITY:** RARE
**NEST TYPE:** CRYSTALLINE
**FLIGHT ABILITY:** 3

# CRYSTAL FOXFIN

**FUN FACT:**
Crystal Foxfin loves to jump in puddles and always makes a splash on rainy days.

**SEASON:** 2
**RARITY:** COMMON
**NEST TYPE:** CRYSTALLINE
**FLIGHT ABILITY:** 2

**DID YOU KNOW?**
Crystal Foxfin has a sweet tooth and likes to go to Citrus Coast!

143

# CRYSTAL POSSWIFT

## FUN FACT:
Crystal Posswift always has her nose in a book—especially if the book is about Hatchtopia!

**SEASON:** 2
**RARITY:** ULTRA RARE
**NEST TYPE:** CRYSTALLINE
**FLIGHT ABILITY:** 4

## DID YOU KNOW?
Crystal Posswift uses a sparkly bookmark made by Crystal Beaveery.

# CRYSTAL OCTAPITTA

## FUN FACT:
Crystal Octapitta scoots her way around Crystal Canyon looking for jewels to add to her growing collEGGtion.

## DID YOU KNOW?
Crystal Octapitta's home is filled with treasure chests!

**SEASON:** 2
**RARITY:** COMMON
**NEST TYPE:** CRYSTALLINE
**FLIGHT ABILITY:** 2

# CRYSTAL CUTIES

# CITRUS COAST

If you wander along Hatchtopia's beautiful shoreline, you may find a **colorful path** that leads to a special place called **Citrus Coast.** It's a sweet spot full of all sorts of tropical delights, where the smell of citrus floats on the breeze. Hatchimals come here to play Hatchy Hopscotch or relax in a hammock while fanning themselves with **Lime Wedge Leaves.**

If the Hatchimals are feeling parched after a long day of playing in the sun, Citrus Coast is the perfect place to quench their thirst. The trees are laden with fruit, and each magnificent tree grows a **special citrus fruit** that's full of flavor. All the Hatchimals have to do is tap a tree to pour a delicious glass of lemonade at the **Sunny Citrus Lemonade Stand!**

The Hatchimals who spend time here love to indulge themselves. They can't get enough of Citrus Coast's tasty juices. In fact, they like them so much that **each Hatchimal's fur sometimes changes** to match the color of their favorite drink!

# CITRUS ANTEAGLE

**FUN FACT:**
Citrus Anteagle loves to take care of his friends. He always wants them to feel relaxed and pampered.

**DID YOU KNOW?**
Citrus Anteagle runs the Citrus Spa!

**SEASON:** 2
**RARITY:** common
**NEST TYPE:** Lime Wedge Leaves
**FLIGHT ABILITY:** 4

# CITRUS BUTTERPUFF

**FUN FACT:**
Citrus Butterpuff brings yummy citrus drinks to Hatchimals flying in Cloud Cove!

**DID YOU KNOW?**
Hatchimals who hang out in Citrus Coast have sparkly bellies from drinking so much juice!

**SEASON:** 2
**RARITY:** common
**NEST TYPE:** GILDED GRAPEFRUIT BARK
**FLIGHT ABILITY:** 5

CITRUS COAST

# CITRUS DRAGGLE

**FUN FACT:**
Citrus Draggle is as bouncy as can be! She's always playing Hatchy Hopscotch!

**DID YOU KNOW?**
Citrus Draggle's favorite drink is Citrus Coast's delicious lemonade!

**SEASON:** 2
**RARITY:** common
**NEST TYPE:** sweet orange tree
**FLIGHT ABILITY:** 3

# CITRUS MOOSEBEAK

**FUN FACT:**
Citrus Moosebeak loves to help. He manages the Sunny Citrus Lemonade Stand.

**DID YOU KNOW?**
Citrus Moosebeak is working on a new drink that combines all the flavors!

**SEASON:** 2
**RARITY:** common
**NEST TYPE:** GILDED GRAPEFRUIT BARK
**FLIGHT ABILITY:** 3

148

# CITRUS NIGHTINGOAT

**FUN FACT:**
Citrus Nightingoat has a bubbly personality. He practically overflows with enthusiasm and excitement.

**DID YOU KNOW?**
Citrus Nightingoat is a taste tester at the lemonade stand!

**SEASON:** 2
**RARITY:** Common
**NEST TYPE:** Sweet Orange Tree
**FLIGHT ABILITY:** 2

# CITRUS SKUNKLE

**FUN FACT:**
Citrus Skunkle has a positive attitude. When life hands her lemons, she makes lemonade.

**DID YOU KNOW?**
Citrus Skunkle loves to bask in the sun!

**SEASON:** 2
**RARITY:** Common
**NEST TYPE:** Lime Wedge Leaves
**FLIGHT ABILITY:** 2

**149**

# FRUITY FAVORITES

# EGGSTRA-SPECIAL COLLEGGTIBLE

Hidden in Hatchtopia's highest mountain ranges is a spot so magical, it can barely be seen in sunlight. Moonlight Mountain reflects a lunar glow and shines a golden light from its peak that can be seen all over the world.

Hatch-legend has it that a very special Hatchimal lives on the mountain, and shares its magical glow. If you're truly lucky, you might just find the rarest Hatchimal of them all: the mysterious Golden Lynx!

## GOLDEN LYNX

**FUN FACT:**
Golden Lynx is nocturnal and can only be seen once the sun has set.

**DID YOU KNOW?**
Golden Lynx loves to hide, so find her if you can!

**SEASON: 2**
**RARITY: LIMITED GOLD EDITION**
**NEST TYPE: LUNAR LEAVES**
**FLIGHT ABILITY: 5**

151

# FRIENDSHIP FARM

When the Hatchimals want some farmyard fun, they head to Friendship Farm. They can tend the **Ruby Radishes** and **Teasing Tomatoes** in the vegetable patch or load up a truck with bales of **Honey Hay** and go for a hayride. And nothing is more fun than going on the rope swing and landing in a big soft pile of Honey Hay!

Friendship Farm is known for its world-famous **dance-a-thons.** Hatchimals come from far and wide to strut their stuff at the Corn Husker Country Dance, Barnyard Ballroom, and Fox-Trotting Fever Contests. Everyone picks a partner, tosses a seed in the vegetable patch for good luck, and then **shakes a tail feather** on the dance floor.

# BREEZY BEACH

Breezy Beach is a **sparkling spot by the sea!** Hatchimals are here for the sunshine, surf, and simple pleasures. Some like to treat themselves to something delicious from the **Oceanside Snack Shack,** while others prefer lounging under a billowing beach umbrella or splashing in the ocean's rolling waves. This hot spot is the perfect place for summer fun!

Breezy Beach is also home to one of the most epic competitions in Hatchtopia: **the Hatchy Games.** Events include the Saltwater Swim, the Seaweed Tug-of-War, the Sand-Castle Contest, and the Hatchtathalon. The competition is fierce, with every Hatchimal in the race striving for success. Winners can earn **Golden Seashell Medals** or try for the grand prize: the **EGG Cup!**

# WISHING STAR WATERFALL

Wishing Star Waterfall lies near the **center of Hatchtopia.** Its enchanted waters flow down from Cloud Cove. During the day, the pool at the bottom of the waterfall sparkles in the sun, and the waterfall itself is filled with sparkling stars. Over time, shooting stars are caught in its waters, giving out a delightful twinkle all day and night!

Each new Hatchimal has one chance to fly to the top of Cloud Cove, ride down the Wishing Star Waterfall, and **make a wish!**

# FABULA FOREST

Leafy and green, Fabula Forest is a sun-dappled spot where Hatchimals come to scamper and play. **Orchid Pine** and **Lavender Oak** trees shade the forest floor, and **Feathered Ferns** provide perfect places for Hatchimals to play Hatch-and-Seek. In Fabula Forest, there's magic hidden everywhere!

Fabula Forest is the place for fun parties and celebrations. There's never a dull moment here! Once a month, the forest plays host to a **Wondrous Woodland Picnic.** Blankets are loaded with heaps of delicious treats, including Winged Watermelon, Sparkle-Me-Sweetcorn, Cackling Cookies, and Camouflaged Cupcakes. Once they have eaten their fill, the Hatchimals have fun with a dance contest. In Fabula Forest, the trees love to play music for the Hatchimals that pass by. They never skip a beat!

# SHIMMERING SANDS

The hottest place in Hatchtopia is Shimmering Sands, where the sun shines brightly over the desert landscape! Shimmering Sands is famous for its silky, sparkling sand dunes. Hatchimals come to cool off in the shade of a **Warming Willow** or a **Piping Palm**. And everyone loves to watch the tumbleweeds roll by as they **sit back and relax!**

Hatchimals from the Savannah and Desert families like to call Shimmering Sands home! Shimmering Sands is also known for its talent show, an entertaining **EGGStravaganza** that lets all the Hatchimals show off their unique skills. Whether they are daring fire-breathers, soulful singers, or bold inventors, all the Hatchimals have a chance to show their friends what makes them **super cool!**

# A WONDROUS WORLD

Hatchtopia is a magical place full of endlessly enchanting delights. From the highest peak in Polar Paradise to the silky sands of Breezy Beach to the lush botanicals of Glittering Garden, there are always surprises in store. Hatchtopia is the perfect place to have an adventure—especially when you've got **Hatchimals friends** by your side!

Now that you've met all the amazing and unique Hatchimals, **it's time to start collEGGting.** Use the note pages and collEGGtor's list to keep track of your collEGGtion. With so many different Hatchimals to meet, you never know who you'll find. But one thing is for sure: You'll find a truly special friend you can love.

## GET READY TO HATCH A WHOLE WORLD!

# COLLEGGTOR'S NOTES

On these pages, you can draw pictures of your Hatchimals, take notes about them, or even write stories about the adventures they have!

COLLEGGTOR'S NOTES

# COLLEGGTOR'S LIST

Use this checklist to help you track
and build your Hatchimals collection.
Are you ready to hatch a whole world?

## GARDEN FAMILY

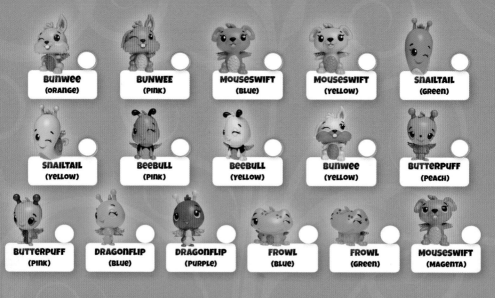

BUNWEE
(ORANGE)

BUNWEE
(PINK)

MOUSESWIFT
(BLUE)

MOUSESWIFT
(YELLOW)

SNAILTAIL
(GREEN)

SNAILTAIL
(YELLOW)

BEEBULL
(PINK)

BEEBULL
(YELLOW)

BUNWEE
(YELLOW)

BUTTERPUFF
(PEACH)

BUTTERPUFF
(PINK)

DRAGONFLIP
(BLUE)

DRAGONFLIP
(PURPLE)

FROWL
(BLUE)

FROWL
(GREEN)

MOUSESWIFT
(MAGENTA)

## FARM FAMILY

LAMBLET
(BLUE)

LAMBLET
(PINK)

PIGPIPER
(PINK)

PIGPIPER
(YELLOW)

PONETTE
(ORANGE)

**PONETTE**
(PINK)

**CHICKCHAFF**
(ORANGE)

**CHICKCHAFF**
(RED)

**DONKEMU**
(BLUE)

**DONKEMU**
(PINK)

**LLAMALOON**
(PINK)

**LLAMALOON**
(PURPLE)

**MACOW**
(ORANGE)

**MACOW**
(WHITE)

**NIGHTINGOAT**
(BLUE)

**NIGHTINGOAT**
(TEAL)

**PONETTE**
(TEAL)

**PONETTE**
(BLUE)

# MEADOW FAMILY

**HEDGYHEN**
(GREEN)

**HEDGYHEN**
(PINK)

**KITTYCAN**
(BLUE)

**KITTYCAN**
(YELLOW)

**PUPPIT**
(BLUE)

**PUPPIT**
(PURPLE)

# JUNGLE FAMILY

**MONKIWI**
(BLUE)

**MONKIWI**
(PINK)

**PANDOR**
(BLUE)

**PANDOR**
(PURPLE)

**TIGRETTE**
(BLUE)

**TIGRETTE**
(ORANGE)

**ALBASLOTH**
(PURPLE)

**ALBASLOTH**
(PINK)

**ANTEAGLE**
(PINK)

**ANTEAGLE**
(PURPLE)

**CHAMELOON**
(BLUE)

**CHAMELOON**
(YELLOW)

**GORILLABEE**
(BLUE)

**GORILLABEE**
(PURPLE)

**PANDOR**
(TEAL)

**PARROO**
(RED)

**TIGRETTE**
(PINK)

**TOUCOO**
(BLUE)

**TOUCOO**
(PINK)

# FOREST FAMILY

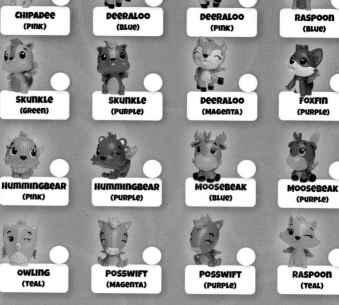

| | | | | |
|---|---|---|---|---|
| **CHIPADEE** (ORANGE) | **CHIPADEE** (PINK) | **DEERALOO** (BLUE) | **DEERALOO** (PINK) | **RASPOON** (BLUE) |
| **RASPOON** (PURPLE) | **SKUNKLE** (GREEN) | **SKUNKLE** (PURPLE) | **DEERALOO** (MAGENTA) | **FOXFIN** (PURPLE) |
| **FOXFIN** (RED) | **HUMMINGBEAR** (PINK) | **HUMMINGBEAR** (PURPLE) | **MOOSEBEAK** (BLUE) | **MOOSEBEAK** (PURPLE) |
| **OWLING** (PINK) | **OWLING** (TEAL) | **POSSWIFT** (MAGENTA) | **POSSWIFT** (PURPLE) | **RASPOON** (TEAL) |

# OCEAN FAMILY

| | | | | |
|---|---|---|---|---|
| **DOLFINCH** (BLUE) | **DOLFINCH** (PINK) | **CRABLER** (RED) | **CRABLER** (YELLOW) | **DOLFINCH** (TEAL) |
| **OCTAPITTA** (BLUE) | **OCTAPITTA** (PINK) | **PENGUALA** (MAGENTA) | **SEASPOON** (BLUE) | **SEASPOON** (PINK) |

# SAVANNAH FAMILY

| | | | | |
|---|---|---|---|---|
| **ELEFLY** (BLUE) | **ELEFLY** (GREEN) | **GIRREO** (PINK) | **GIRREO** (YELLOW) | **LEORIOLE** (ORANGE) |

**LeORIOLe**
(PINK)

**ZeBRUSH**
(PINK)

**ZeBRUSH**
(PURPLe)

**CHeeTRee**
(ORANGe)

**CHeeTRee**
(YeLLOW)

**DRAGGLe**
(PINK)

**eLeFLY**
(PINK)

**GIRReO**
(PURPLe)

**RHOOBY**
(BLue)

**RHOOBY**
(PURPLe)

**ZeBRUSH**
(GReeN)

## DeSeRT FAMILY

**KOALABee**
(BLue)

**KOALABee**
(PURPLe)

**ARMADILLARK**
(GReeN)

**ARMADILLARK**
(YeLLOW)

**CAMeLARK**
(MAGeNTA)

**CAMeLARK**
(YeLLOW)

**KANGAROOSe**
(BLue)

**KANGAROOSe**
(PURPLe)

**SANDSNAKe**
(BLue)

**SANDSNAKe**
(GReeN)

## RIVeR FAMILY

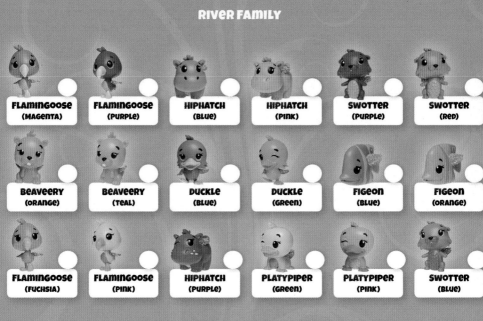

**FLAMINGOOSe**
(MAGeNTA)

**FLAMINGOOSe**
(PURPLe)

**HIPHATCH**
(BLue)

**HIPHATCH**
(PINK)

**SWOTTeR**
(PURPLe)

**SWOTTeR**
(ReD)

**BeAVeeRY**
(ORANGe)

**BeAVeeRY**
(TeAL)

**DUCKLe**
(BLue)

**DUCKLe**
(GReeN)

**FIGeON**
(BLue)

**FIGeON**
(ORANGe)

**FLAMINGOOSe**
(FUCHSIA)

**FLAMINGOOSe**
(PINK)

**HIPHATCH**
(PURPLe)

**PLATYPIPeR**
(GReeN)

**PLATYPIPeR**
(PINK)

**SWOTTeR**
(BLue)

## SPECIAL EDITION POLAR PARADISE

 **POLAR DRAGGLE**

 **POLAR FOXFIN**

 **POLAR HUMMINGBEAR**

 **POLAR PENGUALA**

 **POLAR SEALARK**

 **POLAR SWHALE**

## SPECIAL EDITION LILAC LAKE

 **LILAC BUNWEE**

 **LILAC GIRREO**

 **LILAC HEDGYHEN**

 **LILAC PENGUALA**

 **LILAC SWHALE**

 **LILAC TIGRETTE**

## SPECIAL EDITION GIGGLE GROVE

 **GIGGLING DRAGGLE**

 **GIGGLING ELEFLY**

 **GIGGLING PANDOR**

 **GIGGLING PENGUALA**

 **GIGGLING RASPOON**

 **GIGGLING ZEBRUSH**

## LIMITED EDITION CLOUD COVE

 **CLOUD DRAGGLE**

 **CLOUD KITTYCAN**

 **CLOUD LEORIOLE**

 **CLOUD PIGPIPER**

 **CLOUD PONETTE**

 **CLOUD PUPPIT**

## SPECIAL EDITION SNOWFLAKE SHIRE

 **SNOWFLAKE BELUGULL**

 **SNOWFLAKE HUMMINGBEAR**

 **SNOWFLAKE NARWARBLER**

 **SNOWFLAKE PENGUALA**

 **SNOWFLAKE SEALARK**

 **SNOWFLAKE WALWREN**

# LIMITED EDITION MAGICAL MEADOW

**MAGICAL BUDGIBY** (Yellow)

**MAGICAL BUDGIBY** (Green)

**MAGICAL FARROW** (Pink)

**MAGICAL FARROW** (Green)

**MAGICAL HAMSTAR** (Blue)

**MAGICAL HAMSTAR** (Pink)

**MAGICAL KITTYCAN**

**MAGICAL PUPPIT**

# SPECIAL EDITION GLITTERING GARDEN

**GLITTERING ALBASLOTH**

**GLITTERING CRABLER**

**GLITTERING DUCKLE**

**GLITTERING PLATYPIPER**

**GLITTERING RHOOBY**

**GLITTERING WALWREN**

# SPECIAL EDITION CRYSTAL CANYON

**CRYSTAL BEAVEERY**

**CRYSTAL BUTTERPUFF**

**CRYSTAL CHAMELOON**

**CRYSTAL FOXFIN**

**CRYSTAL POSSWIFT**

**CRYSTAL OCTAPITTA**

# SPECIAL EDITION CITRUS COAST

**CITRUS ANTEAGLE**

**CITRUS BUTTERPUFF**

**CITRUS DRAGGLE**

**CITRUS MOOSEBEAK**

**CITRUS NIGHTINGOAT**

**CITRUS SKUNKLE**

# EGGSTRA-SPECIAL COLLEGGTIBLE

**GOLDEN LYNX**

# INDEX

## PURPLE SKUNKLE

Look out for Purple Skunkle in the Lavender Oaks of the Forest!

**FAMILY: FOREST**
**RARITY: COMMON**
**FLIGHT ABILITY: 2/5**

## PINK OCTAPITTA

Pink Octapitta is a fantastic musician. She plays eight drums at once!

**FAMILY: OCEAN**
**RARITY: RARE**
**FLIGHT ABILITY: 2/5**

## CLOUD LEORIOLE

Cloud Leoriole nests in the snuggly Cashmere Clouds.

**FAMILY: CLOUD COVE**
**RARITY: LIMITED**
**FLIGHT ABILITY: 5/5**

## BLUE KANGAROOSE

You can rely on Blue Kangaroose to always speak her mind!

**FAMILY: DESERT**
**RARITY: COMMON**
**FLIGHT ABILITY: 3/5**